ADIEU
TO EMMANUEL LEVINAS

MERIDIAN

Crossing Aesthetics

Werner Hamacher

& David E. Wellbery

Editors

Translated by
Pascale-Anne Brault
and Michael Naas

*Stanford
University
Press*

—————

*Stanford
California
1999*

ADIEU

TO EMMANUEL LEVINAS

Jacques Derrida

Assistance for the translation was provided
by the French Ministry of Culture.

Originally published in French in 1997 as
Adieu à Emmanuel Levinas
by Editions Galilée
©1997 by Editions Galilée

Stanford University Press
Stanford, California

CIP data appear at the end of the book

Printed and bound in Great Britain by
Marston Book Services Ltd, Oxfordshire

Contents

The translators would like to thank the members of the 1996–97 Levinas Seminar at DePaul University for their help in preparing this translation. Our thanks also to Daniel Price and François Raffoul, who read the entire text and made many fine suggestions, and to Kas Saghafi, whose extraordinary knowledge of Levinas's work was invaluable in preparing notes and checking references. Special thanks to Helen Tartar at Stanford University Press, whose careful and exigent reading improved our work in innumerable ways. We would also like to thank the University Research Council at DePaul University for its generous support of this project. Finally, we owe a great debt of gratitude, once again, to Jacques Derrida, who continues to encourage us, to indulge our queries with patience and kindness, and to grace us with his friendship.

Trans.

Adieu was originally delivered upon the death of Emmanuel Levinas, at the cemetery in Pantin on December 27, 1995.

I would never have dared publish such words, wrenched from me so quickly, in the midst of my sorrow and in the middle of the night, had the initiative not first been taken in the form of a small book edited in Athens (Editions AGRA), in Greek, by Vanghélis Bitsoris with such exacting and generous care. His notes, which are reproduced here, are more than "translator's notes." I thank him first for having written them and then for having translated them into French.

"A Word of Welcome" was given one year later, on December 7, 1996, in the Richelieu Amphitheater of the Sorbonne, at the opening of "Homage to Emmanuel Levinas." Organized by Danielle Cohen-Levinas under the auspices of the Collège International de Philosophie, this gathering lasted two days and went under the title "Face and Sinai."

J.D.

ADIEU

TO EMMANUEL LEVINAS

§ 1 Adieu

For a long time, for a very long time, I've feared having to say *Adieu* to Emmanuel Levinas.

I knew that my voice would tremble at the moment of saying it, and especially saying it aloud, right here, before him, so close to him, pronouncing this word of *adieu*, this word *à-Dieu*, which, in a certain sense, I get from him, a word that he will have taught me to think or to pronounce otherwise.[1]

By meditating upon what Emmanuel Levinas wrote about the French word *adieu*—which I will recall in a few moments—I hope to find a sort of encouragement to speak here. And I would like to do so with unadorned, naked words, words as childlike and disarmed as my sorrow.

Whom is one addressing at such a moment? And in whose name would one allow oneself to do so? Often those who come forward to speak, to speak publicly, thereby interrupting the animated whispering, the secret or intimate exchange that always links one, deep inside, to a dead friend or master, those who make themselves heard in a cemetery, end up addressing *directly, straight on*, the one who, as we say, is no longer, is no longer living, no longer there, who will no longer respond. With tears in their voices, they sometimes speak familiarly to the other who keeps silent, calling upon him without detour or mediation, apostrophizing him, even greeting him or confiding in him. This is not necessarily out of respect for convention, not always simply part of the rhetoric of oration. It is rather so as to traverse speech at the very point where words fail us, since all language that would return to the self, to us, would seem indecent, a reflexive discourse that would end up coming back to the stricken community, to its consolation or its mourning, to what is called, in a confused and terrible expression, "the work of mourning." Concerned only with itself, such speech would, in this return, risk turning away from what is here our law—the law as *straightforwardness* or *uprightness* [*droiture*]: to speak straight on, to address oneself directly *to* the other, and to speak *for* the other whom one loves and admires, before speaking *of* him. To say to him *adieu*, to him, Emmanuel, and not merely to recall what he first taught us about a certain *Adieu*.

This word *droiture*—"straightforwardness" or "uprightness"—is another word that I began to hear otherwise and to learn when it came to me from Emmanuel Levinas. Of all the places where he speaks of uprightness, what first comes to mind is one of his *Four Talmudic Readings*, where uprightness names what is, as he says, "stronger than death."[2]

But let us also keep from trying to find in everything that is said to be "stronger than death" a refuge or an alibi, yet another consolation. To define uprightness, Emmanuel Levinas says, in his commentary on the Tractate Shabbath[3] that consciousness is the "urgency of a destination leading to the Other and not an eternal return to self,"[4]

an innocence without naiveté, an uprightness without stu-
pidity, an absolute uprightness which is also absolute self-
criticism, read in the eyes of the one who is the goal of my
uprightness and whose look calls me into question. It is a
movement toward the other that does not come back to its
point of origin the way diversion comes back, incapable as it
is of transcendence—a movement beyond anxiety and
stronger than death. This uprightness is called *Temimut*, the
essence of Jacob.[5]

This same meditation also sets to work—as each meditation did, though each in a singular way—all the great
themes to which the thought of Emmanuel Levinas has
awakened us, that of responsibility first of all, but of an
"unlimited"[6] responsibility that exceeds and precedes my
freedom, that of an "unconditional yes,"[7] as this text says,
of a "*yes* older than that of naive spontaneity,"[8] a *yes* in accord with this uprightness that is "original fidelity to an
indissoluble alliance."[9] And the final words of this Lesson
return, of course, to death,[10] but they do so precisely so as
not to let death have the last word, or the first one. They
remind us of a recurrent theme in what was a long and incessant meditation upon death, but one that set out on a
path that ran counter to the philosophical tradition extending from Plato to Heidegger. Elsewhere, before saying
what the *à-Dieu* must be, another text speaks of the "extreme uprightness of the face of the neighbor" as the "uprightness of an exposure to death, without defense."[11]

I cannot, nor would I even try to, measure in a few
words the oeuvre of Emmanuel Levinas. It is so large that
one can no longer glimpse its edges. And one would have
to begin by learning once again from him and from *Totality and Infinity*, for example, how to think what an
"oeuvre" or "work"[12]—as well as fecundity—might be.[13]
One can predict with confidence that centuries of read-

ings will set this as their task. We already see innumerable signs, well beyond France and Europe, in so many works and so many languages, in all the translations, courses, seminars, conferences, etc., that the reverberations of this thought will have changed the course of philosophical reflection in our time, and of our reflection *on* philosophy, on what orders it according to ethics, according to another thought of ethics, responsibility, justice, the State, etc., according to another thought of the other, a thought that is newer than so many novelties because it is ordered according to the absolute anteriority of the face of the Other.

Yes, ethics before and beyond ontology, the State, or politics, but also ethics beyond ethics. One day, on the rue Michel-Ange, during one of those conversations whose memory I hold so dear, one of those conversations illuminated by the radiance of his thought, the goodness of his smile, the gracious humor of his ellipses, he said to me: "You know, one often speaks of ethics to describe what I do, but what really interests me in the end is not ethics, not ethics alone, but the holy, the holiness of the holy." And I then thought of a singular separation, the unique separation of the curtain or veil that is given, ordered and ordained [*donné, ordonné*], by God, the veil entrusted by Moses to an inventor or an artist rather than to an embroiderer, the veil that would *separate* the holy of holies in the sanctuary.[14] And I also thought of how other *Talmudic Lessons* sharpen the necessary distinction between sacredness and holiness, that is, the holiness of the other, the holiness of the person, who is, as Emmanuel Levinas said elsewhere, "more holy than a land, even when that land is a Holy Land. Next to a person who has been affronted, this land—holy and promised—is but nakedness and desert, a heap of wood and stone."[15]

This meditation on ethics, on the transcendence of the

holy with regard to the sacred, that is, with regard to the paganism of roots and the idolatry of place, was, of course, indissociable from an incessant reflection upon the destiny and thought of Israel: yesterday, today, and tomorrow. Such reflection consisted of requestioning and reaffirming the legacies not only of the biblical and talmudic tradition but of the terrifying memory of our time. This memory dictates each of these sentences, whether from nearby or afar, even if Levinas would sometimes protest against certain self-justifying abuses to which such a memory and the reference to the Holocaust might give rise.

But refraining from commentaries and questions, I would simply like to give thanks to someone whose thought, friendship, trust, and "goodness" (and I ascribe to this word "goodness" all the significance it is given in the final pages of *Totality and Infinity*)[16] will have been for me, as for so many others, a living source, so living, so constant, that I am unable to think what is happening to him or happening to me today, namely, this interruption or a certain non-response in a response that will never come to an end for me as long as I live.

The non-response: you will no doubt recall that in the remarkable course Emmanuel Levinas gave in 1975–76 (exactly twenty years ago), "La mort et le temps" ("Death and Time"),[17] where he defines death as the patience of time,[18] and engages in a grand and noble critical encounter with Plato as much as with Hegel, but especially with Heidegger, death is often defined—the death that "we meet" "in the face of the Other"[19]—as *non-response*;[20] "It is the without-response," he says.[21] And elsewhere: "There is here an end that always has the ambiguity of a departure without return, of a passing away but also of a scandal ('is it really possible that he's dead?') of non-response and of my responsibility."[22]

Death: not, first of all, annihilation, non-being, or nothingness, but a certain experience for the survivor of the "without-response." Already *Totality and Infinity* called into question the traditional "philosophical and religious" interpretation of death as either "a passage to nothingness" or "a passage to some other existence."[23] It is the murderer who would like to identify death with nothingness; Cain, for example, says Emmanuel Levinas, "must have possessed such a knowledge of death."[24] But even this nothingness presents itself as a "sort of impossibility" or, more precisely, an interdiction.[25] The face of the Other forbids me to kill; it says to me, "Thou shall not kill,"[26] even if this possibility remains presupposed by the interdiction that makes it impossible. This question without response, this question of the without-response, would thus be underivable, primordial, like the interdiction against killing, more originary than the alternative of "To be or not to be,"[27] which is thus neither the first nor the last question. "To be or not to be," another essay concludes, "is probably not the question par excellence."[28]

Today, I draw from all this that our infinite sadness must shy away from everything in mourning that would turn toward nothingness, that is, toward what still, even potentially, would link guilt to murder. Levinas indeed speaks of the survivor's guilt, but it is a guilt without fault and without debt; it is, in truth, an *entrusted responsibility*, entrusted in a moment of unparalleled emotion, at the moment when death remains the absolute ex-ception.[29] To express this unprecedented emotion, the one I feel here and share with you, the one that our sense of propriety forbids us to exhibit, so as to make clear without personal avowal or exhibition how this singular emotion is related to this entrusted responsibility, entrusted as legacy, allow me once again to let Emmanuel Levinas speak, he whose voice I would so much love to hear today when it says that the "death of the other" is the "first death," and that "I am responsible for the other insofar as he is mortal."[30] Or else the following, from the same course of 1975–76:

> The death of someone is not, despite what it might have appeared to be at first glance, an empirical facticity (death as an empirical fact whose induction alone could suggest its universality); it is not exhausted in such an appearance.
>
> Someone who expresses himself in his nakedness—the face—is in fact one to the extent that he calls upon me, to the extent that he places himself under my responsibility: I must already answer for him, be responsible for him. Every gesture of the Other was a sign addressed to me. To return to the classification sketched out above: to show oneself, to express oneself, to associate oneself, *to be entrusted to me*. The Other who expresses himself is entrusted to me (and there is no debt with regard to the Other—for what is due cannot be paid; one will never be even). [Further on it will be a question of a "duty beyond all debt" for the I who is what it is, singular and identifiable, only through the impossibility of being replaced, even though it is precisely here that the "responsibility for the Other," the "responsibility of the hostage," is an experience of substitution[31] and sacrifice.] The Other individuates me in my responsibility for him. The death of the Other affects me in my very identity as a responsible I . . . made up of unspeakable responsibility. This is how I am affected by the death of the Other, this is my relation to his death. It is, in my relation, my deference toward someone who no longer responds, already a guilt of the survivor.[32]

And a bit further on:

> The relation to death in its ex-ception—and, regardless of its signification in relation to being and nothingness, it is an exception—while conferring upon death its depth, is neither a seeing nor even an aiming toward (neither a seeing of being

as in Plato nor an aiming toward nothingness as in Heidegger), a purely emotional relation, moving with an emotion that is not made up of the repercussions of a prior knowledge upon our sensibility and our intellect. It is an emotion, a movement, an uneasiness with regard to the *unknown*.[33]

The *unknown* is emphasized here. The "unknown" is not the negative limit of a knowledge. This non-knowledge is the element of friendship or hospitality for the transcendence of the stranger, the infinite distance of the other. "Unknown" is the word chosen by Maurice Blanchot for the title of an essay, "Knowledge of the Unknown,"[34] which he devoted to the one who had been, from the time of their meeting in Strasbourg in 1923, a friend, the very friendship of the friend.

For many among us, no doubt, certainly for myself, the absolute fidelity, the exemplary friendship of thought, the *friendship* between Maurice Blanchot and Emmanuel Levinas was a grace, a gift; it remains a benediction of our time, and, for more reasons than one, a good fortune that is also a blessing for those who have had the great privilege of being the friend of either of them. In order to hear once again today, right here, Blanchot speak for Levinas, and with Levinas, as I had the good fortune to do when in their company one day in 1968, I will cite a couple of lines. After having named what in the other "ravishes" us, after having spoken of a certain "rapture"[35] (the word often used by Levinas to speak of death),[36] Blanchot says:

But we must not despair of philosophy. In Emmanuel Levinas's book [*Totality and Infinity*]—where, it seems to me, philosophy in our time has never spoken in a more sober manner, putting back into question, as we must, our ways of thinking and even our facile reverence for ontology—we are called upon to become responsible for what philosophy essentially is, by welcoming, in all the radiance and infinite exigency proper to it, the idea of the Other, that is to say, the relation with *autrui*. It is as though there were here a new departure in philosophy and a leap that it, and we ourselves, were urged to accomplish.[37]

If the relation to the other presupposes an infinite separation, an infinite interruption where the face appears, what happens, where and to whom does it happen, when another interruption comes at death to hollow out even more infinitely this first separation, a rending interruption at the heart of interruption itself? I cannot speak of interruption without recalling, like many among you, no doubt, the anxiety of interruption I could feel in Emmanuel Levinas when, on the telephone, for example, he seemed at each moment to fear being cut off, to fear the silence or disappearance, the "without-response," of the other, to whom he called out and held on with an "*allo, allo*" between each sentence, sometimes even in mid-sentence.

What happens when a great thinker becomes silent, one whom we knew living, whom we read and reread, and also heard, one from whom we were still awaiting a response, as if such a response would help us not only to think otherwise but also to read what we thought we had already read under his signature, a response that held everything in reserve, and so much more than what we thought we had already recognized there?

This is an experience that, as I have learned, would remain for me interminable with Emmanuel Levinas, as with all thoughts that are sources, for I will never stop beginning or beginning anew to think with them on the basis of the new beginning they give me, and I will begin again and again to rediscover them on just about any subject. Each time I read or reread Emmanuel Levinas, I am overwhelmed with gratitude and admiration, over-

whelmed by this necessity, which is not a constraint but a
very gentle force that obligates, and obligates us not to
bend or curve otherwise the space of thought in its respect
for the other, but to yield to this other, heteronymous curvature[38] that relates us to the completely other (that is, to
justice, as he says somewhere in a powerful and formidable ellipsis: the relation to the other, that is to say, justice),[39] according to the law that thus calls us to yield to
the other infinite precedence of the completely other.

It will have come, like this call, to disturb, discreetly
but irreversibly, the most powerful and established
thoughts of the end of this millennium, beginning with
those of Husserl and Heidegger, whom Levinas introduced into France some sixty-five years ago! Indeed, this
country, whose hospitality he so loved (and *Totality and
Infinity* shows not only that "the essence of language is
goodness" but that "the essence of language is friendship
and hospitality"),[40] this hospitable France, owes him,
among so many other things, among so many other significant contributions, at least two irruptive events of
thought, two inaugural acts that are difficult to measure
today because they have been incorporated into the very
element of our philosophical culture, after having transformed its landscape.

First, to say it all too quickly, beginning in 1930 with
translations and interpretative readings, there was the initial introduction of Husserlian phenomenology, which
would feed and fecundate so many French philosophical
currents. Then—in truth, simultaneously—there was the
introduction of Heideggerian thought, which was no less
important in the genealogy of so many French philosophers, professors, and students. Husserl and Heidegger at
the same time, beginning in 1930.

I wanted last night to reread a few pages from this

prodigious book,[41] which was for me, as for many others before me, the first and best guide. I picked out a few sentences that have made their mark in time and that allow us to measure the distance he will have helped us cover. In 1930, a young man of twenty-three said in the preface that I reread, smiling, smiling at him: "The fact that in France phenomenology is not a doctrine known to everyone has been a constant problem in the writing of this book."[42] Or again, speaking of the so very "powerful and original philosophy"[43] of "Mr. Martin Heidegger, whose influence on this book will often be felt,"[44] the same book also recalls that "the problem raised here by transcendental phenomenology is an ontological problem in the very precise sense that Heidegger gives to this term."[45]

The second event, the second philosophical tremor, I would even say, the happy traumatism that we owe him (in the sense of the word "traumatism" that he liked to recall, the "traumatism of the other"[46] that comes from the Other), is that, while closely reading and reinterpreting the thinkers I just mentioned, but so many others as well, both philosophers such as Descartes, Kant, and Kierkegaard, and writers such as Dostoevsky, Kafka, Proust, etc.—all the while disseminating his words through publications, teaching, and lectures (at the Ecole Normale Israélite Orientale, at the Collège Philosophique, and at the Universities of Poitiers, Nanterre, and the Sorbonne)— Emmanuel Levinas slowly displaced, slowly bent according to an inflexible and simple exigency, the axis, trajectory, and even the order of phenomenology or ontology that he had introduced into France beginning in 1930. Once again, he completely changed the landscape without landscape of thought; he did so in a dignified way, without polemic, at once from within, faithfully, and from very far away, from the attestation of a completely other place. And I believe that what occurred there, in this second sailing, this second time that leads us back even further than the first, is a discreet but irreversible mutation, one of those powerful, singular, and rare provocations in history that, for over two thousand years now, will have ineffaceably marked the space and body of what is more or less, in any case something different from, a simple dialogue between Jewish thought and its others, the philosophies of Greek origin or, in the tradition of a certain "Here I am,"[47] the other Abrahamic monotheisms. This happened, this mutation happened, *through him*, through Emmanuel Levinas, who was conscious of this immense responsibility in a way that was, I believe, at once clear, confident, calm, and modest, like that of a prophet.

One indication of this historical shock wave is the influence of this thought well beyond philosophy, and well beyond Jewish thought, on Christian theology, for example. I cannot help recall the day when, listening to a lecture by André Neher at a Congress of Jewish Intellectuals, Emmanuel Levinas turned to me and said, with the gentle irony so familiar to us: "You see, he's the Jewish Protestant, and I'm the Catholic"—a quip that would call for long and serious reflection.

In everything that has happened here through him, thanks to him, we have had the good fortune not only of receiving it while living, from him living, as a responsibility entrusted by the living to the living, but also the good fortune of owing it to him with a light and innocent debt. One day, speaking of his research on death and of what it owed to Heidegger at the very moment when it was moving away from him, Levinas wrote: "It distinguishes itself from Heidegger's thought, and it does so in spite of the debt that every contemporary thinker owes to Heidegger—a debt that one often regrets."[48] The good fortune of our debt to Levinas is that we can, thanks to him, assume it and affirm it without regret, in a joyous innocence of admiration. It is of the order of the unconditional *yes* of which I spoke earlier, and to which it responds, "Yes." The regret, my regret, is not having said this to him enough, not having shown him this enough in the course of these thirty years, during which, in the modesty of silences, through brief or discreet conversations, writings too indirect or reserved, we often addressed to one another what I would call neither questions nor answers but, perhaps, to use another one of his words, a sort of "question, prayer," a question-prayer that, as he says, would be anterior to all dialogue.[49]

The question-prayer that turned me toward him perhaps already shared in the experience of the *à-Dieu* with which I began. The greeting of the *à-Dieu* does not signal the end. "The *à-Dieu* is not a finality," he says, thus challenging the "alternative between being and nothingness," which "is not ultimate." The *à-Dieu* greets the other beyond being, in what is "signified, beyond being, by the word 'glory.'"[50] "The *à-Dieu* is not a process of being: in the call, I am referred back to the other human being through whom this call signifies, to the neighbor for whom I am to fear."[51]

But I said that I did not want simply to recall what he entrusted to us of the *à-Dieu,* but first of all to say *adieu* to him, to call him by his name, to call his name, his first name, what he is called at the moment when, if he no longer responds, it is because he is responding in us, from the bottom of our hearts, in us but before us, in us right before us—in calling us, in recalling to us: *à-Dieu.*

Adieu, Emmanuel.

§ 2 A Word of Welcome

Welcome [*bienvenue*], yes, welcome.

On the threshold of this gathering around Emmanuel Levinas, from Emmanuel Levinas, in the trace of his thought and under the double sign "Face and Sinai," it is a word of welcome, yes, a word of welcome that I will thus dare to pronounce.

I do not, of course, venture this in my name alone; nothing would permit me to do so.

Such a greeting might nonetheless be conveyed.

It would attempt to pass from one to another, from someone—him or her—to another, letting itself be received but also heard and interpreted, listened to or questioned. It would seek its passage through the violence of the host, who always keeps watch over the rite. For the risk is great. To dare to say welcome is perhaps to insinuate that one is at home here, that one knows what it means to be at home, and that at home one receives, invites, or offers hospitality, thus appropriating for oneself a place to *welcome* [*accueillir*] the other, or, worse, *welcoming* the other in order to appropriate for oneself a place and then speak the language of hospitality—of course, I have no more intention than anyone else of doing this, though I'm already concerned about the danger of such a usurpation.

For I wish to put before you, at the opening of this conference, a few modest and preliminary reflections on the word "welcome" [*accueil*], as Levinas, it seems to me, has put his mark upon it, having first reinvented it, in those places where he invites us—that is, gives us to think— what is called "hospitality."

Though the honor of delivering this first word of welcome was undeserved, there are several reasons why I felt compelled to accept it. The first has to do with the Collège International de Philosophie, with its history and its memory—and with what I have had to do with it. It was here at the Collège, which thankfully took the initiative to organize this conference, that Emmanuel Levinas spoke in such an unforgettable way. Moreover, from the very beginning—and I can bear witness to this—Emmanuel Levinas gave his support to this institution. I remember visiting him on the rue Michel-Ange in 1982 at the time we were preparing to found the Collège. I had gone there to ask for his advice, his approbation, and even for a promise of participation.

Emmanuel Levinas gave me all of that. He was with us from the very beginning. His thought remains, for so many philosophers, writers, and friends of the Collège, an inspiration or a horizon. Numerous works have been devoted to him within our institution in the form of lectures and seminars. Indeed, one would have to speak here of a constant *study*, in all the respectable senses of this word, in the Latin sense, in the Hebraic sense it translates, and in a sense that is still completely new. It was thus appropriate that the Collège should, as a sign of fidelity, on the first anniversary of the death of Emmanuel Levinas, mark this moment of studious recollection [*recueillement*] in living thought. I take this opportunity, then, to thank in our name the present directors of the Collège, its president François Jullien and especially Danielle Cohen-Levinas, program director, for having taken it upon themselves to respond to our shared hopes for such a gathering.

We are also grateful to the chancellor of the Universities of Paris for the welcome, yes, the welcome that she has extended to us in this venerable place of teaching. It was right here, in the Richelieu Amphitheater, that this thinker who was not only a great professor at the Sorbonne, but a master, once taught.

This master never separated his teaching from a strange and difficult thought of teaching—a magisterial teaching[1] in the figure of *welcoming*, a welcoming where ethics interrupts the philosophical tradition of giving birth and foils the ruse of the master who feigns to efface himself behind the figure of the midwife. For the *study* of which we are speaking cannot be reduced to a maieutics, which would reveal to me only what I am already capable of, as Levinas says. To weave together the themes I would like to privilege here, and to cross the semantic and etymological resources of a word Levinas uses so often, the word *même* ["self, same"], a word whose philology is not his prime concern, we might perhaps say, following *Totality and Infinity*, that maieutics teaches me nothing. It reveals nothing to me. It unveils only what I am already *in a position* [*à même*] to know *myself* [*moi-même*] (*ipse*), capable of knowing [*pouvoir savoir*] by *myself,* in this place where the *self,* the *same* [*même*] (*egomet ipse, medisme, meïsme,* from *metipse, metipsimus*) gathers *in itself* capacity and knowing, power and knowledge, and as the *same* [*même*], the same *being-in-a-position-to* [*être-à même-de*], in the property of what is proper to it, in its very [*même*] essentiality. And perhaps—we will return to this—what is thus announced is a certain appropriating interpretation, indeed a politics of hospitality, a politics of *capacity*, of *power* [*pouvoir*], with regard to the *hôte*, be he the one welcoming (*host*) or the one being welcomed (*guest*).[2] Power *of* the *hôte over* the *hôte*, of the host over the guest or vice versa. The *hosti-pet-s* is the "guest-master," says Benveniste regarding a chain that would link, like two sovereign powers, hospitality and ipseity.[3]

Now, for Levinas, the welcoming of teaching gives and receives something else, more than me and more than some other thing. "To approach the Other in discourse," we read already in the opening pages of *Totality and Infinity*,

> is to *welcome* [I take the liberty of emphasizing this word] his expression, in which at each instant he overflows the idea a thought would carry away from it. It is therefore to *receive* [Levinas's emphasis] from the Other beyond the capacity of the I, which means exactly: to have the idea of infinity. But this also means: to be taught. The relation with the Other, or Discourse, is a non-allergic relation, an ethical relation; but inasmuch as it is *welcomed* [my emphasis again] this discourse is a teaching. But teaching does not come down to maieutics; it comes from the exterior and brings me more than I contain.[4]

If I felt I had to accept the great and undue honor of delivering these first words, it was also—something more difficult to admit—because I felt myself incapable of preparing for today a lecture worthy of the name, worthy of this conference, and worthy of Levinas. When Danielle Cohen-Levinas extended me this honor, I agreed to be the first to speak so as, of course, to take part in this homage, something I deeply wished to do, but also so as to efface myself as quickly as possible on the threshold of hospitality. I hoped then to be able to remain silent, protected by this alibi—and especially to listen. I will indeed do this, but not before drawing out at some length—and I beg your forgiveness in advance—an interpretation of welcoming or hospitality. I will do so in the name or under the title of the *opening*, since it was agreed that that would be the general title given to this introduction.

~

Now, in a first reversal, Levinas suggests thinking the opening in general on the basis of hospitality or welcoming, and not the other way around. He does so explicitly. These two words, "opening" and "hospitality," are at once associated and dissociated in his work. They obey a subtle law. Like every law, it calls for cautious deciphering.

How is one to interpret this hospitality *in the name* of Levinas? How might one do so by speaking, not in his place and in his name, but along with him, speaking with him as well, first by listening to him today, by coming to places where, in order to recall their names to them, he re-named, made renowned, Sinai and the face, "Sinai" and "face"? These names were brought together for the sake of this gathering, but do we know how to hear them? In what language? As common or proper nouns? As translated from another language? From the past of a holy writing or from an idiom to come?

On the horizon of these preliminary reflections, I will be guided by a question that I will in the end leave in suspense, being content simply to situate some of its premises and points of reference. It would concern, on first view, the relationships between an *ethics* of hospitality (an ethics *as* hospitality) and a *law* or a *politics* of hospitality, for example, in the tradition of what Kant calls the conditions of universal hospitality in *cosmopolitical law*: "with a view to perpetual peace."

The classical form of this question would perhaps be found in the figure of a founding or legitimating foundation. It might be asked, for example, whether the ethics of hospitality that we will try to analyze in Levinas's thought would be able to found a law and a politics, beyond the familial dwelling, within a society, nation, State, or Nation-State.

This question is no doubt serious, difficult, and necessary, but it is already canonical. We will try to subordinate it to another suspensive question, to what might be called a sort of *epochē*. Which one?

Let us assume, *concesso non dato*, that there is no assured passage, following the order of a foundation, according to a hierarchy of founding and founded, of principial originarity and derivation, between an ethics or a first philosophy of hospitality, on the one hand, and a law or politics of hospitality, on the other. Let us assume that one cannot *deduce* from Levinas's ethical discourse on hospitality a law and a politics, some particular law or politics in some determined situation today, whether close to us or far away (assuming that we could even evaluate the distance separating the Church of St. Bernard [in Paris] from Israel, from the former Yugoslavia, from Zaire or Rwanda).[5] How, then, are we to interpret this impossibility of founding, of deducing or deriving? Does this impossibility signal a failing? Perhaps we should say the contrary. Perhaps we would, in truth, be put to another kind of test by the apparent negativity of this lacuna, by this hiatus between ethics (first philosophy or metaphysics—in the sense, of course, that Levinas has given to these words), on the one hand, and, on the other, law or politics. If there is no lack here, would not such a hiatus in effect require us to think

law and politics otherwise? Would it not in fact open—
like a hiatus—both the mouth and the possibility of another speech, of a decision and a responsibility (juridical
and political, if you will), where decisions must be made
and responsibility, as we say, *taken*, without the assurance
of an ontological foundation? According to this hypothesis, the absence of a law or a politics, in the strict and determined sense of these terms, would be just an illusion.
Beyond this appearance or convenience, a return to the
conditions of responsibility and of the decision would im-
pose itself, between ethics, law, and politics. Such a return
might be undertaken, as I will try to suggest in conclusion, according to two very close, but perhaps heterogeneous, paths.

I

Has anyone ever noticed? Although the word is neither
frequently used nor emphasized within it, *Totality and Infinity* bequeaths to us an immense treatise *of hospitality*.

This is borne out less by the occurrences of the word
"hospitality," which are, in fact, rather rare, than by the
links and discursive logic that lead to this vocabulary of
hospitality. In the concluding pages, for example, hospitality becomes the very name of what opens itself to the
face, or, more precisely, of what "welcomes" it. The face
always lends itself to a welcome, and the welcome welcomes only a face, the face that should be our theme today, but that, as we know from reading Levinas, must
elude all thematization.

This irreducibility to a theme, this exceeding of all
thematizing formalization or description, is precisely
what the face has in common with hospitality. Levinas is
not content to distinguish hospitality from thematiza-

tion; as we will hear in a moment, he explicitly opposes them.

When he completely redefines intentional subjectivity, submitting subjection to the idea of infinity in the finite, he multiplies in his own way propositions in which a noun defines a noun. The substantive-subject and the substantive-predicate might then exchange places in the proposition, which would upset at once the grammar of de-termination and traditional logical writing, right up to its dialectical affiliation. For example: "It [intentionality, consciousness of . . .] is attention to speech or welcome of the face, *hospitality* and not thematization."[6]

If I was tempted to underscore the word *hospitality* in this sentence, I must now—so as to efface it—go back on this pedagogical or rhetorical concern. For all the concepts that are opposed to "thematization" are at once synonymous and of equal value. None of them should be privileged, and thus underscored. Before going any further in the interpretation of this proposition, we should note what silently justifies such an apposition. It seems to follow a sort of élan, content simply to unfold, to explicate. It appears to proceed, indeed to leap, from one synonym to the next. Though it appears as such only once, the "or" (*vel*) of substitution could be inscribed between each noun—excluding, of course, "thematization": "It [intentionality, consciousness of . . .] is *attention* to *speech* or *welcome* of the *face*, *hospitality* and not thematization."

The word "hospitality" here translates, brings to the fore, re-produces, the two words preceding it, "attention" and "welcome." An internal paraphrase, a sort of periphrasis, a series of metonymies that bespeak hospitality, the face, welcome: tending toward the other, attentive intention, intentional attention, *yes* to the other. Intentionality, attention to speech, welcome of the face, hospitality—all these are the same, but the same as the welcoming of the other, there where the other withdraws from the theme. This movement without movement effaces itself in the welcoming of the other, and since it opens itself to the infinity of the other, an infinity that, as other, in some sense precedes it, the welcoming *of* the other (objective genitive) will already be a response: the *yes to* the other will already be responding to the welcoming *of* the other (subjective genitive), to the *yes* of the other. This response is called for *as soon as* the infinite—always *of* the other— is welcomed. We will follow its trace in Levinas. But this "as soon as" does not mark the moment or threshold of a beginning, of an *archē*, since infinity will already have been pre-originarily welcomed. Welcomed in anarchy. This responsible response is surely a *yes*, but a *yes to* preceded by the *yes of* the other. One should no doubt extend without limit the consequences of what Levinas asserts in a passage where he repeats and interprets the idea of infinity in the Cartesian *cogito*: "It is not I, it is the other that can say *yes*."[7]

(If one were to pursue these consequences with the necessary temerity and rigor, they would perhaps lead to another way of thinking the responsible decision. Levinas would probably not say it in this way, but could it not be argued that, without exonerating myself in the least, decision and responsibility are always *of the other*? They always come back or come down to the other, from the other, even if it is the other in me?[8] For, in the end, would an initiative that remained purely and simply "mine" still be a decision, in accordance with the most powerful tradition of ethics and philosophy, which requires that the decision always be "my" decision, the decision of one who can freely say "as for myself, I," *ipse, egomet ipse*? Would what comes down to me in this way still be a decision? Do we have the right to give the name "decision" to a purely autonomous movement, even if it is one of welcoming or hospitality, that would proceed only from me, by me, and would simply deploy the possibilities of a subjectivity that is mine? Would we not be justified in seeing here the unfolding of an egological immanence, the autonomic and automatic deployment of predicates or possibilities proper to a subject, without the tearing rupture that should occur in every decision we call free?

If it is only the other who can say *yes*, the "first" *yes*, the welcome is always the welcome *of* the other. One must then think the grammars and genealogies of this genitive. If I put quotation marks around the "first" of the "first" *yes*, it was to accede to a scarcely thinkable hypothesis: there is no *first yes*, the *yes* is already a response. But since everything must begin with some *yes*, the response begins, the response commands. We must make the best of this aporia, into which we, finite and mortal, are *thrown* and without which there would be no promise of a path. It is necessary to *begin by responding*. There would thus be, in the beginning, no first word. The call is called only from the response. The response comes ahead of or comes to encounter the call, which, before the response, is first only in order to await the response that makes it come. Despite all the tragic objections that this harsh law might seem to justify ["but then what?," it might be said; "What about the call with no response, the solitary cry of distress? And the solitude of prayer, and the infinite separation to which it attests, would this not be, to the contrary, the true condition of the call, of the infinitely finite call?"], the necessity remains, as imperturbable as death, that is to say, the necessity of finitude: from the depthless depths of its solitude, a call can only itself be heard, can only hear itself, and hear itself calling, from the promise of a response. We are speaking here of the call as such, if there is one. For if one wants to appeal to a call that is not even recognized, that does not recognize itself, as a call, one can, at least to think it, do without any response. This is always possible, and it no doubt does not fail to happen.

Levinas does not say this, or he does not say it in this way, but I would like to approach him today by way [*voie*] of this non-way.)

Though the word "hospitality" occurs relatively seldom in *Totality and Infinity*, the word "welcome" is unarguably one of the most frequent and determinative words in that text. This could be verified, even if, to my knowledge, it has not been done. More operational than thematic, this concept operates everywhere in order to speak of the first gesture in the direction of the Other.

But is this welcome even a gesture? It is, rather, the first movement, an apparently passive movement, but the *right* or *good* movement. The welcome cannot be derived, no more than the face can, and there is no face without welcome. It is as if the welcome, just as much as the face, just as much as the vocabulary that is co-extensive and thus profoundly synonymous with it, were a first language, a set made up of quasi-primitive—and quasi-transcendental— words. We must first think the possibility of the welcome in order to think the face and everything that opens up or is displaced with it: ethics, metaphysics or first philosophy, in the sense that Levinas gives to these words.

The welcome determines the "receiving," the receptivity of receiving as the ethical relation. As we have already heard: "To approach the Other in discourse is to welcome his expression, in which at each instant he overflows the idea a thought would carry away from it. It is therefore to *receive* from the Other beyond the capacity of the I."

This to *receive*, a word underscored here and proposed

as a synonym of to *welcome*, receives only to the extent, an extent beyond all measure, that it receives beyond the capacity of the I. As we will see, this dissymmetrical disproportion will later mark the law of hospitality. But in an unexpected proposition within the same paragraph, reason is itself *interpreted* as this hospitable receptivity. The long line of the philosophical tradition that passes through the concept of receptivity or passivity, and thus, it was thought, of sensibility as opposed to rationality, is here reoriented at its most basic level.

It is a question of the acceptation of reception.

One can apprehend or perceive the meaning of to *receive* only on the basis of the hospitable welcome, the welcome opened or offered to the other. Reason itself is a *receiving*. Another way of saying it, if one still wishes to speak within the law of the tradition, though against it, against its inherited oppositions, is that reason *is* sensibility. Reason itself is a welcome inasmuch as it welcomes the idea of infinity—and the welcome is rational.

Is it insignificant that Levinas speaks in this place of a *door* [*porte*]? Is the place that he designates in this way simply a trope in a rhetoric of hospitality? If the figure of the door, on the threshold that opens the at-home [*chez-soi*], were a "manner [*façon*] of speaking," this would suggest that speech is a *manner* of speaking, a manner of doing or *managing* [*faire*] with one's hand held out, addressing oneself to the Other so as to give him something to eat or drink, or to allow him to breathe, as Levinas so often recalls elsewhere. The open door, as a manner of speaking, calls for the opening of an exteriority or of a transcendence of the idea of infinity. This idea comes to us through a door, and the door passed through is none other than reason in teaching.

In the same passage of "Transcendence as the Idea of

Infinity," the scrupulous precautions of "but," "yet," and "without" sharpen the originality of this *receiving* and this *welcome*. This open door is anything but a simple passivity, anything but an abdication of reason:

> To approach the Other in discourse is to *welcome* [my emphasis] his expression, in which at each instant he overflows the idea a thought would carry away from it. It is therefore to *receive* [Levinas's emphasis] from the Other beyond the capacity of the I, which means exactly: to have the idea of infinity. *But* this also means: to be taught. The relation with the Other, or Discourse, is a non-allergic relation, an ethical relation; *but* inasmuch as it is *welcomed* [my emphasis again] this discourse is a teaching. *But* [third "but," my emphasis, a *but* within a *but* (*mais dans le mais*), *magis*, but even more, even better] teaching does not come down to [*ne revient pas à*] maieutics; it comes from the exterior and brings me more than I contain. [It does not come back, or come down to— it comes, and comes from elsewhere, from the exterior, from the other.] In its non-violent transitivity the very epiphany of the face is produced. The Aristotelian analysis of the intellect, which discovers the agent intellect *coming in by the door* [my emphasis here and in the following], absolutely exterior, and *yet* constituting, *without* in any way compromising, the sovereign activity of reason, already substitutes for maieutics a transitive action of the master, since reason, without abdicating, is found to be in a position to *receive* [*à même de recevoir*] [Levinas's emphasis].

Reason *in a position to receive*: what can this hospitality of reason give, this reason as *the capacity to receive* [*pouvoir recevoir*] ("*in a position to receive*"), this reason under the law of hospitality? This reason as the law of hospitality? Levinas underscores, for a second time in the same paragraph, the word "receive." In this vein, as we know, he will undertake the most daring analyses of receptivity, of a passivity before passivity, analyses whose stakes will become more and more decisive precisely where the words seem to get carried away and become disidentified in a discourse that opens each signification to its other (relation *without* relation, passivity *without* passivity, "passivity . . . more passive than every passivity,"[9] etc.)

The word "welcome" comes up again on the same page. It designates, along with the "notion of the face," the opening of the I and the "philosophical priority of the existent over Being."[10] This thought of welcoming thus also initiates a discreet but clear and firm contestation of Heidegger, indeed of the central motif of gathering oneself, of recollection [*recueillement*], or of gathering together (*Versammlung*), of the collecting (*colligere*) that would be accomplished in recollection. There is, of course, a thinking of recollection in Levinas, particularly in the section of *Totality and Infinity* entitled "The Dwelling." But such recollection of the "at home with oneself [*chez-soi*]" already assumes the welcome; it is the *possibility of welcoming* and not the other way around. It makes the welcome possible, and, in a sense, that is its sole destination. One might then say that the welcome to come is what makes possible the recollection of the at home with oneself, even though the relations of conditionality appear impossible to straighten out. They defy chronology as much as logic. The welcome also, of course, supposes recollection, that is, the intimacy of the *at home with oneself* and the figure of woman, feminine alterity. But the welcome [*l'accueil*] would not be a secondary modification of collecting [*cueillir*], of this *col-ligere* that is not without link or ligature to the origin of religion, to this "relation without relation" for which Levinas *reserves*, as he says, the word "religion" as the "ultimate structure": "For the relation between the being here below and the transcendent being that results in no community of concept or totality—a relation without relation—we reserve the term religion."[11] The *possibility* of the welcome would thus come—so as to open them up—*before* recollection, even *before* collecting, before the act from which everything nonetheless seems to be derived. Levinas says elsewhere that "to possess the idea of infinity is to have already welcomed the Other"[12] and that "to welcome the Other is to put in question my freedom."[13]

Among the numerous occurrences of the word *welcome* in *Totality and Infinity*, let us recall for the moment the one at the beginning of the chapter "Truth and Justice" that defines nothing less than Discourse: Discourse as Justice. Discourse presents itself as Justice "in the uprightness of the *welcome* made to the face."[14]

With this word "Justice" are announced all the formidable problems that we will try to address later, notably those that arise with the third. The third arrives without waiting. Without waiting, the third comes to affect the experience of the face in the face to face. Although this interposition of the third does not interrupt the welcome itself, this "thirdness" [*tertialité*] turns or makes turn toward it, like a witness (*terstis*) made to bear witness to it, the dual [*duel*] of the face to face, the singular welcome of the unicity of the other. The illeity of the third is thus nothing less, for Levinas, than the beginning of justice, at once as law and beyond the law, in law beyond the law. *Otherwise than Being or Beyond Essence* speaks of this "*illeity*, in the third person, but according to a 'thirdness' that is different from that of the third man, from that of the third interrupting the face to face of the welcome of the other man—interrupting the proximity or approach of the neighbor—from that of the third man with whom justice begins."[15]

Earlier, a note specifies that justice is "this very presence of the third."[16] From pages where I have always thought I could make out a certain distress of the aporia, the complaints, attestations, and protestations, along with the outcries or objections, of a Job who would be tempted to appeal not *to* justice but *against* it, come to us the desperate questions of a just man. Of a just man who would like to be more just than justice. Another Job, unless this is the other of Job, asks what he has to do with justice, with just and unjust justice. These questions cry out a contradiction, one that is without equal and without precedent, the terrible contradiction of the Saying by the Saying, Contra-Diction itself:

> The third is other than the neighbor, but also another neighbor, and also a neighbor of the other, and not simply his fellow. What then are the other and the third for one another? What have they done to one another? Which passes before the other? . . . The other and the third, my neighbors, contemporaries of one another, put distance between me and the other and the third. "Peace, peace to the neighbor and the one far-off" (Isaiah 57: 19)—we now understand the point of this apparent rhetoric. The third introduces a contradiction in the Saying. . . . It is of itself the limit of responsibility and the birth of the question: What do I have to do with justice? A question of conscience, of consciousness. Justice is necessary, that is, comparison, coexistence, contemporaneousness, assembling . . . [17]

Levinas does not shrink from analyzing the consequences of this "is necessary." It reintroduces us, as if by force, into places ethics should exceed: the visibility of the face, thematization, comparison, synchrony, system, copresence "before a court of justice." In truth, it does not re-introduce us in a secondary way into these places but calls us back to them from before the time before. For the third does not wait; it is there, from the "first" epiphany of the face in the face to face.

The question, then, is the third.

The "birth of the question" is the third. Yes, the *birth*, for the third does not wait; it comes at the origin of the face and of the face to face. Yes, the birth of the *question as question*, for the face to face is immediately suspended, interrupted without being interrupted, *as* face to face, as the dual of two singularities. The ineluctability of the third is the law of the question. The question of a question, as addressed to the other and from the other, the other of the other, the question of a question that is surely not first (it comes after the *yes* to the other and the *yes* of the other) though nothing precedes it. No thing, and especially no one.

The question, but also, as a result, justice, philosophical intelligibility, knowledge, and even, announcing itself gradually from one person to the next, from neighbor to neighbor, the figure of the State. For, as we will hear, all this *is necessary*.

The same logic, the same sentences, often the literal repetition of these statements, lead Levinas in "Peace and Proximity" to deduce from this ineluctability of the third *at once* the origin of the question itself (and thus of philosophical discourse, whose status is governed and whose signature legitimated by the question: almost the entirety of Levinas's discourse, for example, almost the entire space of its intelligibility for us, appeals to this third)[18] *and* justice *and* the "political structure of society." The leap without transition, the rupturing mutation of the "without question" at the birth of the "first question," defines at the same time the passage from ethical responsibility to juridical, political—and philosophical—responsibility. It also indicates the move out of immediacy:

Doubtless, responsibility for the other human being is, in its *immediacy, anterior to every question*. But how does responsibility obligate if a third troubles this exteriority of two where my subjection of the subject is subjection to the neighbor? The third is other than the neighbor but also another neighbor, and also a neighbor of the other, and not simply their fellow. What am I to do? What have they already done to one another? Who passes before the other in my responsibility? What, then, are the other and the third with respect to one another? *Birth of the question.*

The first question in the interhuman is the *question of justice. Henceforth it is necessary to know*, to become consciousness. Comparison is superimposed onto my relation with the *unique* and the incomparable, and, in view of equity and equality, a weighing, a thinking, a calculation, the *comparison of incomparables*, and, consequently, the neutrality—presence or representation—of being, the thematization and the visibility of the face.[19]

The deduction proceeds in this way right up to "the political structure of society, subject to laws," right up to "the dignity of the citizen," where, however, a sharp distinction must remain between the ethical subject and the civic one.[20] But this move out of purely ethical responsibility, this interruption of ethical immediacy, is itself immediate. The third does not wait; its illeity calls from as early as the epiphany of the face in the face to face. For the absence of the third would threaten with violence the purity of ethics in the absolute immediacy of the face to face with the unique. Levinas does not say it in exactly this way, but what is he doing when, beyond or through the dual of the face to face between two "uniques," he appeals to justice, affirming and reaffirming that justice "is necessary," that the third "is necessary"? Is he not trying to take into account this hypothesis of a violence in the pure and immediate ethics of the face to face? A violence potentially unleashed in the experience of the neighbor and of absolute unicity? The impossibility of discerning here between good and evil, love and hate, giving and taking, the desire to live and the death drive, the hospitable welcome and the egoistic or narcissistic closing up within oneself?

The third would thus protect against the vertigo of ethical violence itself. For ethics could be doubly exposed to such violence: exposed to undergo it but also to exercise it. Alternatively or simultaneously. It is true that the protecting or mediating third, in its juridico-political role, violates in its turn, at least potentially, the purity of the ethical desire devoted to the unique. Whence the terrible ineluctability of a double constraint.

Though Levinas never puts it in these terms, I will risk pointing out the necessity of this *double bind* in what follows from the axioms established or recalled by Levinas: if the face to face with the unique engages the infinite ethics of my responsibility for the other in a sort of *oath before the letter*, an unconditional respect or fidelity, then the ineluctable emergence of the third, and, with it, of justice, would signal an initial perjury [*parjure*].[21] Silent, passive, painful, but inevitable, such perjury is not accidental and secondary, but is as originary as the experience of the face. Justice would begin with this perjury. (Or at least justice as law; even if justice remains transcendent or heterogeneous to law, these two concepts must not be dissociated: justice *demands* law, and law does not wait any more than does the illeity of the third in the face. When Levinas says "justice," we are also authorized to hear "law," it seems to me. Law [*droit*] would begin with such a perjury; it would betray ethical uprightness [*droiture*].)

To my knowledge, *perjury* is not a theme in Levinas, nor is *oath*—and I do not recall having come across or noticed these words in the writings that concern us. Whence the necessity of specifying an "oath before the letter," which would also mean, and this time we would be very close to the letter of Levinas's text, a debt before every contract or loan. For Levinas does not hesitate to speak of a "primordial word of honor," precisely in the experience of "bearing witness," of the "attestation of oneself," of the "uprightness of the face to face."[22]

An intolerable scandal: even if Levinas never puts it this way, justice commits perjury as easily as it breathes; it betrays the "primordial word of honor" and swears [*jurer*] only to perjure, to swear falsely [*parjurer*], swear off [*abjurer*] or swear at [*injurier*]. It is no doubt in facing this ineluctability that Levinas imagines the sigh of the just: "What do I have to do with justice?"

Henceforth, in the operation of justice one can no longer distinguish between fidelity to oath and the perjury of false witness, and even before this, between betrayal and betrayal, always more than one betrayal. One should then, with all requisite analytical prudence, respect the quality, modality, and situation of these breaches of the sworn word, of this "primordial word of honor" before all oaths. But such differences would never efface the trace of the inaugural perjury. Like the third who does not wait, the proceedings that open both ethics and justice are in the process of committing quasi-transcendental or originary, indeed, pre-originary, perjury. One might even call it *ontological*, once ethics is joined to everything that exceeds and betrays it (ontology, precisely, synchrony, totality, the State, the political, etc.). One might even see here an irrepressible evil or a radical perversion, were it not that bad intentions or bad will might be absent here, and were its possibility, at least the haunting of its possibility,[23] a sort of pervertibility, not also the condition of the Good, of Justice, Love, Faith, etc. And of perfectibility.

This spectral "possibility" is not, however, the abstraction of a liminal pervertibility. It would be, rather, the *impossibility* of controlling, deciding, or determining a limit, the *impossibility* of situating, by means of criteria, norms, or rules, a tenable threshold separating pervertibility from perversion.

This impossibility *is necessary.* It is necessary that this threshold not be at the disposal of a general knowledge or a regulated technique. It is necessary that it exceed every regulated procedure in order to open itself to what always risks being perverted (the Good, Justice, Love, Faith—and perfectibility, etc.). This is necessary, this possible hospitality to the worst is necessary so that good hospitality can have a chance, the chance of letting the other come, the *yes* of the other no less than the *yes* to the other.

These infinite complications do not change anything about the general structure from which they are, in truth, derived: discourse, justice, ethical uprightness have to do first of all with *welcoming*. The welcome is always a welcome reserved for the face. A rigorous study of this thought of welcoming should not only highlight all the contexts in which the recurrence of this word imposes itself in a regulated way.[24] An enormous task. It would also need to take into account the chances or opportunities offered it by the French idiom: the idiom, an ambiguous chance, the *shibboleth* of the threshold, the preliminary chance of hospitality, one for which Levinas was grateful, a chance for his writing but also a chance granted by his philosophical writing to the French language. These chances accumulate places appropriate to the crypt; they also enrich the difficulties one encounters in translating the vocabulary of welcoming into other languages, as when, for example, this analysis of hospitality (hospitality of a language and welcome offered to a language, language of the *hôte*, of the host, and language as *hôte*, as guest) allows us to notice, in the collection or recollection of meaning, the extremely significant play between *recollection* [*recueillement*] and *welcome* [*accueil*].

As we noted a moment ago, Levinas always opens recollection upon welcoming. He recalls the opening of recollection by the welcome, the welcome of the other, the welcome reserved for the other. "Recollection refers to a welcome," he says in a passage from "The Dwelling" that would call for a long, interrogatory analysis. There Levinas describes the intimacy of the home or of the "at home" [*chez-soi*]: these are places of gathered interiority, of recollection, certainly, but a recollection in which the hospitable welcome is accomplished. After an analysis of an inapparent phenomenon, *discretion*, which combines manifestation and withdrawal in the face, he names Woman: "the other whose presence is discreetly an absence, with which is accomplished the *hospitable welcome par excellence* which describes the field of intimacy, is the Woman. The woman is the condition for recollection, the interiority of the Home, and inhabitation."[25]

What *bearing* [*portée*] does this recollection have? Logically speaking, of course, as we have just heard, it "refers to a welcome." It bears on this; this is its *ference*, its *rapport* or relation. But it is *apparently*—in the figure of the Woman or the Home, in the I-Thou of "a silent language," of "an understanding without words," of "an expression in secret," in what Levinas here calls "feminine alterity"—but one modality of welcoming.

This feminine alterity seems marked by a series of lacks. A certain negativity is implied in the words "without," "not," and "not yet." What is lacking here is nothing less than an eminent possibility of language: not language in general but the *transcendence* of language, words and teaching that come from the height of the face:

> The simple living from . . . the spontaneous agreeableness of the elements is *not yet* habitation. But habitation is *not yet* the transcendence of language. The Other who *welcomes* in intimacy is *not* the *you* [*vous*] of the face that reveals itself in a dimension of height, but precisely the *thou* [*tu*] of familiarity: a language *without* teaching, a silent language, an understanding *without* words, an expression in secret. The I-Thou in which Buber sees the category of interhuman relationship is the relation not with the interlocutor but with feminine alterity.[26]

If this feminine alterity thus seems to lack the "height" of the face, the absolute verticality of the Most-High in teaching, she nonetheless speaks—and speaks a human language. There is nothing of the animal in her, even if certain signs in the description might seem to point in this direction. This language is simply "silent," and if there is hospitality here, "a land of asylum or refuge," it is because the dwelling goes beyond animality. If the at home with oneself of the dwelling is an "at home with oneself as in a land of asylum or refuge," this would mean that the inhabitant also dwells there as a refugee or an exile, a guest and not a proprietor. That is the humanism of this "feminine alterity," the humanism of the other woman, of the other (as) woman. If woman, in the silence of her "feminine being," is not a man, she remains [*demeure*] human. The familiarity of the home does not bring separation to an end, no more than proximity in general does, and no more than love or eros implies fusion. Familiarity accomplishes, on the contrary, "the *en-ergy* of separation":

> With it [that is, with familiarity] separation is constituted as dwelling and inhabitation. To exist henceforth means to

dwell. To dwell is not the simple fact of the anonymous reality of a being cast into existence as a stone one casts behind oneself; it is a *recollection*, a coming to oneself, a retreat home with oneself as in a *land of asylum or refuge*, which answers to a *hospitality*, an expectancy, a *human welcome*. In *human welcome* the language that keeps silence remains an essential possibility. Those silent comings and goings of the feminine being whose footsteps reverberate the secret depths of being are not the turbid mystery of the animal and feline presence whose strange ambiguity Baudelaire likes to evoke.[27]

This is, it would appear, one of the contexts for the discussion of Buber's I-Thou relation. (Despite Levinas's reservations regarding Buber's discourse on "thou-saying" [*tutoiement*], he sometimes acknowledges in such "thou-saying" an "exceptional uprightness.")[28] But how can one think that this is just one context among others? How can one believe that this modality of welcoming remains simply one determinate modality of hospitality concerning the home, the dwelling, and especially the femininity of woman? Levinas's formulations would be enough to warn us against such a restriction. At least they complicate the logic in a singular way, for they insistently and explicitly define "Woman" as "hospitable welcome par excellence," "the feminine being" as "the welcoming one par excellence," "welcoming in itself."[29] They underscore this essential determination in a movement whose consequences we will not cease to measure. In at least two directions.

First, we must think that "the welcoming one par excellence," "the welcoming in itself," welcomes within the limits that we have just recalled, that is, those of inhabitation and feminine alterity (*without* the "transcendence of language," *without* the "height" of the face in teaching, etc.). The danger is that these limits risk dividing, not the ethical from the political, but, even before this, the pre-ethical—"inhabitation" or "feminine alterity" before the transcendence of language, the height and illeity of the face, teaching, etc.—*from* the ethical, as if there could be a welcoming, indeed a welcoming "par excellence," "in itself," *before* ethics. And as if the "feminine being" as such did not as yet have access to the ethical. The situation of the chapter "The Dwelling" and, even more, the place of the section to which it belongs ("Interiority and Economy") would thus pose serious architectonic problems, that is, were architectonics not an "art of the system" (Kant) and were *Totality and Infinity* not to begin by calling into question systemic totality as the supreme form of philosophical exposition. For architectonics perhaps always leads philosophy back into the habitability of habitation: it is always the interiority of an economy that already poses the problems of welcoming that confront us here.

Is it not from this abyss that we must now try to interpret the writing, language (languages), and composition of this singular book, and in it the exposition of welcoming, of welcoming par excellence, on the basis of sexual difference? We have not yet exhausted these questions, especially since they also concern the section "Beyond the Face," beginning with "The Ambiguity of Love" and everything that touches upon femininity in the analysis of the caress ("Phenomenology of Eros").

We cannot take up these questions here. Let us simply note, for now, that "Phenomenology of Eros" remains first of all and only *turned*, so to speak, toward the feminine, oriented, therefore, from a masculine *point of view*, but from a *point of view* that goes blindly (with no view [*point de vue*]) into this place of non-light that would be "The Feminine" insofar as it is "essentially violable and inviolable."[30] This inviolable violability, this vulnerability of a being that prohibits violence at the very place it is exposed to it without defense, is what, in the feminine, seems to figure the face itself, even though the feminine "presents a face that goes beyond the face," where eros "consists in going beyond the possible."[31]

We should never minimize the stakes—or the risks—of these analyses. They seem, in 1961, to be still borne along by the élan of analyses Levinas had already devoted to eros in 1947 in *Existence and Existents* and *Time and the Other*.[32] The feminine there names what allows one to transcend, in a single movement, at once the ego and the world of light, and thus a certain phenomenological domination extending from Plato to Husserl. Hence, the feminine, which in *Totality and Infinity* will be "the welcoming one par excellence," is already defined, in 1947, as "the other par excellence."

> The world and light are solitude. . . . It is not possible to grasp the alterity of the Other, which is to shatter the definitiveness of the ego, in terms of any of the relationships which characterize light. Let us anticipate a moment, and say that the plane of *eros* allows us to see that the other par excellence is the feminine. . . . *Eros*, when separated from the Platonic interpretation which completely fails to recognize the role of the feminine, can be the theme of a philosophy which, detached from the solitude of light, and consequently from phenomenology properly speaking, will concern us elsewhere.[33]

During the same period, in *Time and the Other*,[34] an analysis of sexual difference (which Levinas insistently reminds us is not one difference among others, one type or species of the genre "difference": neither a contradiction nor a complementarity) leads to analogous propositions. The feminine is a "mode of being that consists in slipping away from the light," a "flight before light," a "way of existing" in the "hiding" of modesty.

If these remarks of 1947 in effect announce *Totality and Infinity* (1961), Levinas will revisit certain of these propositions many years later, in 1985. We will return to this.

Levinas must begin by distinguishing, in short, between hospitality and love, since the latter does not accomplish the former. But he nonetheless acknowledges that "the transcendence of discourse is bound to love." Since the transcendence of discourse is not transcendence itself, this creates a tangle that is difficult to undo. Certain threads go at once *further* and *less far* than others. Just as with architectonics, an objective topology would remain powerless to sketch out the lines, surfaces, and volume, the angles and cornerstones. It would seek in vain to make out the lines of demarcation, to measure the distances. What sort of extent are we talking about here? What goes "further" than language, namely, love, also goes "less far" than it.

But all the threads undeniably pass through the knot of hospitality. There they are tied together, and there they come undone: "The metaphysical event of transcendence—*the welcome of the Other, hospitality*—Desire and language—is not accomplished as Love. But the transcendence of discourse is bound to love. We shall show how in love transcendence goes both further and less far than language."[35]

As for the second direction referred to a moment ago, we must be reminded of this implacable law of hospitality: the *hôte* who receives (the host), the one who welcomes the invited or received *hôte* (the guest), the welcoming *hôte* who considers himself the owner of the place, is in truth a *hôte* received in his own home. He receives the hospitality that he offers *in* his own home; he receives it *from* his own home—which, in the end, does not belong to him. The *hôte* as host is a guest. The dwelling opens itself to itself, to its "essence" without essence, as a "land of asylum or refuge." The one who welcomes is first welcomed in his own home. The one who invites is invited by the one whom he invites. The one who receives is received, receiving hospitality in what he takes to be his own home, or indeed his own land, according to a law that Rosenzweig also recalled. For Rosenzweig emphasized this originary dispossession, this withdrawal by which the "owner" is expropriated from what is most his own, the *ipse* from its ipseity, thus making of one's home a place or location one is simply passing through:

> even when it has a home, this people [the eternal people], in recurrent contrast to all other peoples on earth, is not allowed full possession of that home. It is only "a stranger and a sojourner." God tells it: "This land is mine." The holiness of the land removed it from the people's spontaneous reach.[36]

Though the relationship between these propositions of Rosenzweig and those of Levinas might appear forced or arbitrary, I believe it necessary, and I will continue to put it to work, at least implicitly, to relate, on the one hand, this divine law that would make of the inhabitant a guest [*hôte*] received in his own home, that would make of the owner a tenant, of the welcoming host [*hôte*] a welcomed guest [*hôte*], and, on the other, this passage about the feminine being as "the welcoming one par excellence," as "welcoming in itself." For Levinas thus defines the welcoming one himself, or rather, *her*self, welcoming in itself—and thus that on the basis of which welcoming could be announced in general—at a precise moment: at the moment when he deems it necessary to emphasize that the home is not owned. Or at least it is owned, in a very singular sense of this word, only insofar as it is already hospitable to its owner. The head of the household, the master of the house, is already a *received hôte*, already a *guest* in his own home. This absolute precedence of the welcome, of the welcoming, of welcom*ing* [*accueillance*], would be precisely the femininity of "Woman," interiority as femininity—and as "feminine alterity." As in the story by Klossowski, assuming that this reference to a scene of perversion is not too shocking here, the master of the house becomes the guest of his guest because, first of all, the woman is there. The experience of pervertibility of which we spoke above, which at once calls for and excludes the third, here appears indissociably linked to sexual difference.

More than one reading could be given of the few lines I am about to cite. It would be necessary to linger awhile in their vicinity. One approach would be to acknowledge, so as then to question, as I once did in a text to which I do not wish to return here,[37] the traditional and androcentric attribution of certain characteristics to woman (private interiority, apolitical domesticity, intimacy of a sociality that Levinas refers to as a "society without language,"[38] etc.). But another reading of these lines might be attempted, one that would not oppose in a polemical or dialectical fashion either this first reading or this interpretation of Levinas.

Before situating this other orientation, let us listen again to the definition of the "hospitable welcome par excellence," "the welcoming one par excellence," "welcoming in itself," that is, "the feminine being":

> The home that founds possession is not a possession in the same sense as the movable goods it can collect and keep. It is possessed because it already and henceforth is *hospitable for its owner.* This refers us to its essential interiority, and to the inhabitant that inhabits it *before every inhabitant, the welcoming one par excellence, welcoming in itself—the feminine being.*[39]

The other approach to this description would no longer raise concerns about a classical androcentrism. It might even, on the contrary, make of this text a sort of feminist manifesto. For this text defines the welcome par excellence, the welcome or welcoming of absolute, absolutely originary, or even pre-originary hospitality, nothing less than the pre-ethical origin of ethics, on the basis of femininity. That gesture reaches a depth of essential or meta-empirical radicality that takes sexual difference into account in an ethics emancipated from ontology. It confers the opening of the welcome upon "the feminine being" and not upon the *fact* of empirical women. The welcome, the anarchic origin of ethics, belongs to "the dimension of femininity" and not to the empirical presence of a human being of the "feminine sex." Levinas anticipates the objection:

> Need one add that there is no question here of defying ridicule by maintaining the empirical truth or countertruth that every home *in fact* presupposes a woman? The feminine has been encountered in this analysis as one of the cardinal points of the horizon in which the inner life takes place—and the empirical absence of the human being of "feminine sex" in a dwelling nowise affects the dimension of femininity which remains open there, as the very welcome of the dwelling.[40]

Need one choose here between two incompatible readings, between an androcentric hyperbole and a feminist one? Is there any place for such a choice in ethics? And in justice? In law? In politics? Nothing is less certain. Without stopping for the moment at this alternative, let us simply keep the following in mind for the trajectory we are suggesting here: whatever we might speak about later, and whatever we might say about it, we would do well to remember, even if silently, that this thought of welcome, there at the opening of ethics, is indeed marked by sexual difference. Such sexual difference will never again be neutralized. The absolute, absolutely originary welcome, indeed, the pre-original welcome, the welcoming par excellence, is feminine; it takes place in a place that cannot be appropriated, in an open "interiority" whose hospitality the master or owner receives before himself then wishing to give it.

Hospitality thus precedes property, and this will not be without consequence, as we will see, for the taking-place of the gift of the law, for the extremely enigmatic relationship between refuge and the Torah, the city of refuge, the land of asylum, Jerusalem, and the Sinai.

II

We will not be able to carry out here a task that is nonetheless so necessary: to patiently explore this thought of welcome along every path of its writing, everywhere it itself follows a trace, writing itself out according to the phrasing or idiom of Levinas, to be sure, but at the intersection of many languages, with a fidelity to more than one memory.

Let us thus approach more modestly what is announced when the word "hospitality," this quasi-synonym of "welcome," nonetheless comes to determine or perhaps restrict its features, thereby pointing out to us, between ethics, politics, and law, certain places, places of the "birth of the question," as we noted a moment ago, "places" to which it would perhaps be appropriate to assign the names "face" and "Sinai," as they have been suggested for our study today.

The sentence whose reading I interrupted and digressed from a few moments ago ("It [intentionality, consciousness of . . .] is attention to speech or welcome of the face, hospitality and not thematization") proposes a series of equivalences. But what is the copula doing in this serial proposition? It binds together phenomena of unbinding [*déliaison*]. It assumes that this approach of the face—as intentionality or welcome, that is, as hospitality—remains inseparable from separation itself. Hospitality assumes "radical separation" as experience of the alterity of the other, as relation to the other, in the sense that Levinas emphasizes and works with in the word "relation," that is, in its ferential, referential or, as he sometimes notes, deferential *bearing* [*portée*]. The relation to the other is deference. Such separation signifies the very thing that Levinas re-names "metaphysics": ethics or first philosophy, as opposed to ontology. Because it opens itself to—so as to welcome—the irruption of the idea of infinity in the finite, this metaphysics is an experience of hospitality. Levinas thereby justifies the arrival of the word *hospitality*; he prepares the threshold for it. The passage *meta ta physika* passes through the hospitality of a finite threshold that opens itself to infinity, but this *meta-physical* passage takes place, it comes to pass and passes through the abyss or the transcendence of separation:

> To metaphysical thought, where a finite has the idea of infinity—where radical separation and relationship with the other are produced simultaneously—we have reserved the term intentionality, consciousness of . . . It is attention to speech or welcome of the face, hospitality and not thematization.

The logical articulations of these propositions work once again like so many elliptical and peaceful acts of force. The predicative copula of the "is" adjoins and links concepts according to the law of a certain separation, an infinite separation without which there would be no hospitality worthy of the name.

What does this mean? A deliberate terminological decision assigns the word "metaphysical" to a situation where
"a finite has the idea of infinity"; it claims the right to
"reserve" the use of a word ("To metaphysical thought,
where a finite has the idea of infinity . . . we have *reserved*
the term intentionality, consciousness of . . . "). Earlier,
the synchrony of a "simultaneously," which had come
to determine the auto-production of an event that "is
produced" or that "produces itself," equates metaphysics,
the welcome of the other, and "radical separation" ("To
metaphysical thought, where a finite has the idea of infinity—where the radical separation is *produced* and, *simultaneously*, the relation with the other—we have *reserved* the
term intentionality, consciousness of . . . "; my emphasis,
of course). The sentence that follows ("It is attention to
speech or welcome of the face, hospitality and not thematization") retains the discreet gentleness of what some
might nonetheless interpret as the logic of performative
decrees attempting to invent a new language or a new use
for old words. It opens up hospitality by an act of force
that is nothing other than a declaration of peace, the declaration of peace itself. We will ask later on what the event
of peace is for Levinas.

The paradoxical use of a copula ("It *is* attention to
speech or welcome of the face, hospitality and not thematization") not only establishes between several substantive
significations an essential bond that stems precisely from
the common unbinding of a radical separation. The copula also bears us toward what will be explicitly situated, a
few pages later, "beyond Being." Such a proposition might
henceforth put forward as hospitality not only intentionality or consciousness of . . . , to which the grammar of the
"it" and all the appositions that follow clearly refer, but
metaphysics itself, infinity in the finite, radical separation,

the relation with the other, etc. The essance[41] of what is or, rather, of what *opens* beyond being is hospitality.

One might draw from this a rather abrupt conclusion, in a language that is no longer literally that of Levinas: hospitality is infinite or it is not at all; it is granted upon the welcoming of the idea of infinity, and thus of the unconditional, and it is on the basis of its opening that one can say, as Levinas will a bit further on, that "ethics is not a branch of philosophy, but first philosophy."[42]

Now, how can this infinite and thus unconditional hospitality, this hospitality at the opening of ethics, be regulated in a particular political or juridical practice? How might it, in turn, regulate a particular politics or law? Might it give rise to—keeping the same names—a politics, a law, or a justice for which none of the concepts we have inherited under these names would be adequate? To deduce from the presence in my finitude of the idea of infinity that consciousness *is* hospitality, that the *cogito* is a hospitality offered or given, an infinite *welcome*, is a step that the French knight who walked at such a good pace would perhaps not so easily have taken, even if Levinas often appeals to him.[43]

Because intentionality is hospitality, it resists thematization. An act without activity, reason as receptivity, a sensible *and* rational experience of *receiving*, a gesture of welcoming, a welcome offered to the other as stranger, hospitality opens as intentionality, but it cannot become an object, thing, or theme. Thematization, on the contrary, already presupposes hospitality, welcoming, intentionality, the face. The closing of the door, inhospitality, war, and allergy already imply, as their possibility, a hospitality offered or received: an original or, more precisely, pre-originary declaration of peace. Here is perhaps one of the most formidable traits in the logic of an extremely complex relation with the Kantian legacy that—as we will see—distinguishes ethical or originary peace (originary but not natural: it would be better to say pre-originary, an-archic), according to Levinas, from "perpetual peace" and from a universal, cosmo-*political*, and thus political and juridical hospitality, the hospitality that Kant reminds us must be instituted in order to interrupt a bellicose state of nature, to break with a nature that knows only actual or virtual war. Instituted as peace, universal hospitality must, according to Kant, put an end to natural hostility. For Levinas, on the contrary, allergy, the refusal or forgetting of the face, comes to inscribe its secondary negativity against a backdrop of peace, against the backdrop of a hospitality that does not belong to the order of the political, or at least not simply to a political space. Here is perhaps a second difference from Kant. Whereas the Kantian concept of peace is apparently juridical and political, the correlate of an inter-state and republican institution, Levinas, at the end of "Politics After!," puts forward the suggestion (and "suggestion" is his word, just about the last one of "Politics After!") that "peace is a concept that goes beyond purely political thought."[44] A distant but faithful echo of the declaration of peace that opens the Preface of *Totality and Infinity*: "Of peace there can be only an eschatology."

Like a short treatise on "war and peace," this Preface also removes the concept of prophetic eschatology from its usual philosophical applicability, from the horizon of history or of an end of history. This peace of which there can be only an eschatology "does not take place in the objective history disclosed by war, as the end of that war or as the end of history."[45]

Let us temporarily abandon these few indicative references. They were intended simply to justify, though from afar, the necessity of going back to the extraordinary complexity of this problematic, in Kant and in Levinas, between the Kant of *Toward Perpetual Peace* [*Zum ewigen Frieden*] and the question of the ethical, the juridical, and the political in Levinas's thought of hospitality.

Intentionality is hospitality, then, says Levinas quite literally. The force of this copula carries hospitality very far. There is not some intentional experience that, here or there, would or would not undergo the circumscribed experience of something that would come to be called, in a determining and determinable fashion, hospitality. No, intentionality opens, from its own threshold, in its most general structure, as hospitality, as welcoming of the face, as an ethics of hospitality, and, thus, as ethics in general. For hospitality is not simply some region of ethics, let alone, and we will return to this, the name of a problem in law or politics: it is ethicity itself, the whole and the principle of ethics. And if hospitality does not let itself be circumscribed or derived, if it originarily conveys the whole of intentional experience, then it would have no contrary: the phenomena of allergy, rejection, xenophobia, even war itself would still exhibit everything that Levinas explicitly attributes to or allies with hospitality. He insisted on underscoring this, it seems to me, in an interview where he said, though I cannot recall his exact words, that the worst torturer attests—since he does not save it—to the very thing that he destroys, in himself or in the other, namely, the face. Whether it wants to or not, whether we realize it or not, hostility still attests to hospitality: "radical separation," "relation with the other," "intentionality, consciousness of . . . , attention to speech or welcome of the face."

In other words, there is no intentionality before and without this welcoming of the face that is called hospitality. And there is no welcoming of the face without this discourse that is justice, "the uprightness of the *welcome* made to the face," as these words from the final pages of *Totality and Infinity* affirm: "the essence of language is goodness, or again, . . . the essence of language is friendship and hospitality."[46]

Reciprocally, one would understand nothing about hospitality without clarifying it through a phenomenology of intentionality, a phenomenology that renounces, however, *where necessary*, thematization. That is indeed a mutation, a leap, a radical but discreet and paradoxical heterogeneity introduced into phenomenology by the ethics of hospitality. Levinas also interprets it as a singular interruption, a suspension or *epochē of* phenomenology itself, even more and even earlier than a phenomenological *epochē*.

It is tempting to relate this interruption to the one that introduces radical separation, that is to say, the condition of hospitality. For the interruption marked by ethical discourse *on the inside* of phenomenology, in its inside-outside, is like no other. Phenomenology imposes this interruption upon itself; it *interrupts itself.* This interruption of the self by the self, if such a thing is possible, can or must be taken up by thought: this is ethical discourse— and it is also, as the limit of thematization, hospitality. Is not hospitality an interruption of the self?

(A *certain* interruption of phenomenology by itself already imposed itself upon Husserl, though he did not, it is true, take note of it as an ethical necessity. This happened when it became necessary to renounce the principle of principles of originary intuition or of presentation in person, "in the flesh." That this became necessary in the *Cartesian Meditations* precisely when it was a question of the other, of an *alter ego* that never makes itself accessible except by way of an appresentational analogy and so remains radically separated, inaccessible to originary perception, is not insignificant for either Husserlian phenomenology or Levinas's discourse on the transcendence of the Other—a discourse that has also in its own way inherited this interruption. What is said here of the other cannot be separated, as we have insisted elsewhere, from alterity as the movement of temporalization. In other words, "Time and the Other," to cite a title.)

One will understand nothing about hospitality if one does not understand what "interrupting oneself" might mean, the interruption of the self by the self as other. A note in "Proximity" makes this clear by speaking of "ethical language, which phenomenology resorts to in order to mark its own interruption."[47] This ethical language "does not come from an ethical intervention laid out over descriptions. It is the very meaning of approach, which contrasts with knowing."

The interruption is not imposed on phenomenology as if by decree. In the very course of phenomenological description, following an intentional analysis faithful to its movement, its style, and its norms, the interruption *is produced* (*by itself*) [*se produit*]. It *is decided* (*by itself*) [*se décide*] in the name of ethics, as interruption of the self by the self. Interruption of the self by a phenomenology that gives itself over to its own necessity, to its own law, right where this law orders it to interrupt thematization, which also means to be unfaithful to itself out of fidelity to itself, out of this fidelity "to intentional analysis" that Levinas always claimed.[48] This fidelity that makes one unfaithful is the respect for consciousness of . . . as hospitality.

Levinas himself considers this interruption of self to be a "paradox." This paradox translates the "enigma" of a face that presents itself, if one can say this, only at the point where, withdrawing in discretion, it is "refractory to disclosure or unveiling and manifestation," if not to the light of "glory." What thus turns out to be interrupted, rather than torn or lifted up, sublated, in the first moment of hospitality is nothing less than the figure of the veil and of truth as revelation, as unveiling or even as veiling/unveiling. This note from "Proximity" was called for by an analysis of the "face as a trace," which "indicates its own absence in my responsibility" and "requires a description that can be formed only in ethical language."

This ethical language of phenomenology describes prescription at the point where prescription lets itself be described only by already prescribing, by still prescribing. One can always interpret phenomenological discourse as at once prescription and the neutral description of the fact of prescription. This neutralization always remains possible, and is always to be feared. It is no doubt one of the dangers Levinas is trying to fend off each time he criticizes neutralization or neutrality—the one he imputes to Heidegger and, curiously, credits Blanchot with having "contributed to bring out."[49]

Through a series of analytical propositions relating hospitality to the metaphysics of the face, a redefinition of the subjectivity of the subject names in passing welcoming, habitation, and the home. These themes, we recall, are treated earlier in *Totality and Infinity* under the title "The Dwelling,"[50] where Levinas speaks of the "at home with oneself" beyond the "for oneself," of the "land of asylum or refuge" and, before all else, of the feminine: "feminine alterity," welcome par excellence, gentleness of the feminine face, feminine language that keeps silent in the discretion of a silence that has nothing natural or animal-like about it, etc.

If the category of the *welcome* everywhere determines an opening that would come even before the première, before the opening, it can never be reduced to an indeterminate figure of space, to some sort of aperture or opening to phenomenality (for example, in the Heideggerian sense of *Erschliessung, Erschlossenheit,* or *Offenheit*). The welcome orients, it *turns* the *topos* of an opening of the door and of the threshold toward the other;[51] it offers it to the other *as* other, where the *as such* of the other slips away from phenomenality, and, even more so, from thematicity. The vocabulary of welcoming, the noun "welcome" and the verb "to welcome," thus everywhere and with an exceptional frequency provide the keys, as it were, to this book. In the "Conclusions," for example: "In the welcome made to the Other I welcome the Most High to which my freedom is subordinated."[52]

The subordination of freedom indicates a subjection of the *subjectum,* certainly, but a subjecting that, rather than depriving the subject of its birth and its freedom, actually gives [*donne*] it its birth, along with the freedom that is thereby ordained [*ordonnée*]. It is still a question of subjectivation, but not in the sense of interiorization; rather, the subject comes to itself in the movement whereby it welcomes the Wholly Other as the Most High. This subordination ordains [*ordonne*] and gives [*donne*] the subjectivity of the subject. The welcome of the Most High in the welcome of the Other is subjectivity itself. The paragraph that we began to read ("It is attention to speech or welcome of the face, hospitality and not thematization") comes together in conclusion in a sort of theorem or definitional proposition. It ends by re-defining subjectivity as hospitality, separation without negation and thus without exclusion, aphoristic energy of the unbinding [*déliaison*] in ethical affirmation: "It [self-consciousness "in its home"] thus accomplishes separation positively, without being reducible to a negation of the being from which it separates. But thus precisely it can welcome that being. The subject is a host."[53]

The subject: a host. A startling equation, and it would not take much, it seems to me, to make it resonate, consonate, and appear together with another formula that will emerge some years later, in "Substitution" and then in *Otherwise than Being or Beyond Essence.* Just as brief, dense, and aphoristic, this second sentence does not say, or no longer says, "The subject is a host" but "The subject is hostage,"[54] or else, a bit further, "The ipseity . . . is hostage."

Does this amount to the same thing? To the same in the relation to the other? Are these two propositions talking about the same subjectivity of the subject?

This being-"hostage" of the subject surely is not, any more than its being-"host," some late attribute or accident that would supervene upon it. Like the being-host, the being-hostage is the subjectivity of the subject as "responsibility for the Other":

> Responsibility for the Other is not an accident that happens to a subject, but precedes essence in it, has not awaited freedom, in which a commitment to the Other would have been made. I have not done anything and I have always been under accusation—persecuted. The ipseity, in the passivity without archē characteristic of identity, is hostage. The word *I* means *here I am*, answering for everything and for everyone.[55]

What, then, is this formula "The subject is hostage" doing? It is marking a scansion, a strong punctuation in the unfolding of a logic of *sub*stitution. The hostage is first of all someone whose unicity endures the possibility of a *sub*stitution. It undergoes this substitution; it is a subject subjected to it, a subject that submits at the very moment when it presents itself ("here I am") in its responsibility for others. Substitution thus takes over for the "subordination" (the constitution of subjectivity in subjection, in being subjected, in subjectivation) that we just situated in *Totality and Infinity*. Inseparable from a new conceptual and lexical configuration, from new words or words struck with a new impression ("vulnerability," "traumatism," "psychosis," "accusation," "persecution," "obsession," etc.), "substitution" carries forth quite continuously, it seems to me, the élan and the "logic" of *Totality and Infinity*, though it dislodges even more drastically the primacy of intentionality, at least what would still link this primacy to that of a "will" or an "activity." If the illeity of the third always marks, as we saw, the birth of the question at the same time as the "it is necessary" of justice, the word "question" is now forced to adapt to the situation of the hostage: the subject is hostage insofar as it is less a "question" than "*in* question." Its accusation, its persecution, its obsession, its "persecuting obsession" is its "being-in-question." Not the being of the questioner or of the questioned, but the being-in-question, where, so to speak, it *finds itself under accusation* [*mis en cause*], where it passively *finds itself* and finds itself contested, interpellated, implicated, persecuted, *under accusation*. We must thus think—and think as having, in the end, the same aim—this other way of inhabiting, of welcoming or of being welcomed. The host [*hôte*] is a hostage insofar as he is a subject put into question, obsessed (and thus besieged), persecuted, in the very place where he takes place, where, as emigrant, exile, stranger, a guest [*hôte*] from the very beginning, he finds himself elected to or taken up by a residence [*élu à domicile*] before himself electing or taking one up [*élire domicile*].

The subjectivity of a subject is responsibility or being-in-question in the form of the total exposure to offense in the cheek offered to the smiter.[56] This responsibility is prior to dialogue, to the exchange of questions and answers. . . .

The recurrence of persecution in the *oneself* is thus irreducible to intentionality in which, even in its neutrality as a contemplative movement, the will is affirmed. . . . The recurrence of the self in responsibility for others, a persecuting obsession, goes against intentionality, such that responsibility for others could never mean altruistic will. . . . It is in the passivity of obsession, or incarnated passivity, that an identity individuates itself as unique, without recourse to any *system* of references, in the impossibility of evading the assignation of the other without blame. . . . *under* accusation by everyone, the responsibility for everyone goes to the point of substitution. The subject is hostage.[57]

We are moving about here in the obscure environs of a semantic, if not etymological, kinship between *host* and *hostage*, between the subject as host and the subject (or ipseity) as hostage. Whether we understand by the word "hostage" (*ostage*) a guest [*hôte*] given over or received as a substitutive pledge [*gage*] in places of power and at the disposal of a sovereign, or whether we understand *obsidium* or *obsidatus* (the condition of being hostage or captive) on the basis of an obsidional situation, a state of siege, we can, according to both lineages, find a token or proof [*gage*] of substitution ("accusation by everyone," "responsibility for everyone"), that is, the passage Levinas clears between these two figures of the same ethics: hospitality without property and the "persecuting obsession" of the hostage. The genealogy that links the term "ipseity," always at the center of Levinas's discourse, to the semantics of hospitality, to the *hospes* as *hosti-pet-s*, namely, the guest-master, where the significations of the self, of mastery, possession, and power are intertwined in a very tight web, in proximity to the hostility of the *hostis*—this genealogy, which we recalled earlier, is here affirmed.[58]

III

Against the backdrop of these enormous difficulties, we might here, today, note the emergence of at least *three types of question*. We will attempt simply to situate them and then devote very unequal analyses to them—unequal with regard to one another and with regard to what is at stake in each.

~

1. First there is the question of a trajectory, extending over a number of years, between these two brief and explicit definitions of the subject in the form *S is P*: "the subject is host" and "the subject is hostage." Two predicative propositions whose subject remains the subject. Does this at once logical and historical trajectory translate an equivalence? Or does it displace and thereby transform once again a concept of the subject that, already in *Totality and Infinity*, subordinates the ontological tradition to an ethics of hospitality, to a phenomenological analysis of the welcome, to the height of the face?

2. In the course of this trajectory, what becomes of the welcome when the subject-host takes on the attribute of being-hostage, along with all the concepts that here form a chain (substitution of the irreplaceable assigned to its responsibility, "unlimited accusative of persecution," "the self, a hostage . . . already substituted for the others,"[59] "the signification of the pronoun *self* for which our Latin grammars themselves know no nominative form,"[60] debt before any borrowing and before any commitment, responsibility without freedom, traumatism, obsession, persecution, the irreducibility of sacrifice, etc., in other words, the law of the accusative in the welcome)?

Does not such a "reverting"—this is Levinas's word,

and it describes the movement of ethics, the ethical relation—make appear a quasi-moment that would precede any welcoming? The very welcoming that might have appeared up until now originary or even pre-original? What relation is to be established between the hypothesis of this "reverting" and the concepts of election or the political as they were articulated during the same years?

I am unable to develop this second question here, but I will support it, as a question that remains a question, with two references to "Substitution" in *Otherwise than Being*.

A. The first names an election that, in a strange but significant, indeed absolutely exceptional fashion, would *precede* any welcome that the subject might reserve for anything, in particular, for the Good or goodness. The elective assignation chooses me by preceding me and making my capacity to welcome conform to it. This certainly does not contradict what we read in *Totality and Infinity*, where the welcome welcomes beyond itself, where it *must*, in truth, always welcome more than it can welcome. But here, in the assignation of responsibility, the election of the hostage seems not only more "originary" (in truth, as always, more originary than the origin) but violent, indeed traumatizing—more so, it seems, than the sometimes pacifying vocabulary of the welcome and of the hospitality of the host might suggest. Levinas thus speaks, though this is only an example, of

the *difference* in the non-indifference of the Good, which *elects me before I welcome it.* [I emphasize these last words.] It preserves its *illeity* to the point of letting it be excluded from the analysis, save for the trace it leaves in words or the "objective reality" in thoughts, according to the unimpeachable witness of Descartes' Third Meditation. That in the responsibility for another, the ego, already a self, already obsessed by the neighbor, would be unique and irreplaceable is what confirms its election.[61]

Once again "illeity," the emergence of the question, of the third, and of justice, designates *sometimes* the interruption of the face to face, *sometimes* the very transcendence of the face in the face to face, the condition of the *You*, the rupture of the *I-Thou* (and thus of a certain femininity, a certain experience of "feminine alterity") in the proximity of the neighbor. But this "sometimes, sometimes" implies neither an alternative nor a sequentiality: the two movements contend with one another at some time earlier than this "sometimes, sometimes." They do not wait; they do not wait for one another. Already in *Totality and Infinity* Levinas acknowledges this "presence of the third" and the question of justice that emerges *from the first instant*, if we can say this, of the face, as if on the threshold of the face to face: "The third looks at me in the eyes of the Other—language is justice. It is not that there first would be the face, and then the being it manifests or expresses would concern himself with justice. . . . By essence the prophetic word responds to the epiphany of the face . . . the epiphany of the face inasmuch as it attests the presence of the third."[62]

Given the impossible possibility toward which we are thus hurried (the aporia or abyss), this contending without alternative might overdetermine all the questions that assail us here. The contending of a "He [*Il*] in the depth of the You [*Tu*]," a formula by which Levinas relates *three occurrences* [*instances*] that we must endlessly welcome [*accueillir*] together—or recollect [*recueillir*] as the same, yes, the wholly other as the same, the same He, the separated one: *the illeity of the He* ("He in the depth of the You") as the third person, *holiness* and *separation*: "The Desirable is intangible and separates itself from the relationship with Desire which it calls for; through this separation or holiness it remains a third person, the He in the depth of the You."[63]

The meshes or links of this chain bear all their force toward this point of rupture or translation: "ethics," the word "ethics," is only an approximate equivalent, a makeshift Greek word for the Hebraic discourse on the holiness of the separated (*kadosh*). Which is not to be confused—especially not—with sacredness. But in what language is this possible? The welcome of the separated, the movement of the one who becomes separated in welcoming when it becomes necessary to greet the infinite transcendence of a separated holiness, to say *yes* at the moment of a separation, indeed of a departure that is not the contrary of an arrival—is it not this deference that inspires the breath of an *à-Dieu*?

B. The second reference turns us toward another possible meaning for such a "reverting": an excess of the ethical over the political, an "ethics *beyond* the political." What might "beyond" mean in a passage from "Substitution" that takes up what we noted earlier about this "paradox," namely, the interruption *of self*, the interruption of self *in* phenomenology—*by* phenomenology *itself*, which thus surprises and suspends itself at the very moment of taking leave of itself in itself? Ethics beyond the political—that is the paradoxical reverting into which phenomenology would find itself "thrown":

> Phenomenology can follow out the reverting of thematization into anarchy in the description of the approach [that is, the approach as the experience of the welcoming of the other or of the face as a neighbor]. Then ethical language succeeds in expressing the paradox in which phenomenology finds itself abruptly thrown. For *ethics, beyond the political,* is found at the level of this reverting. Starting with the approach, the

description finds the neighbor bearing the trace of a withdrawal that orders it as a face.[64]

"The trace of a withdrawal that orders it as a face": this
withdrawal disjoins time itself. If it were produced only *in*
time, in the time of everyday representation, the withdrawal would come to modify only the presence of the present, the now-present, the past-present, or the future-pre-
sent. But here, this withdrawal, this trace of the face, dislo-
cates the order of temporal presence and representation.
Translated into the vocabulary of hospitality, this trace of
the face, of the visage, would be called *visitation* ("A face is
of itself a visitation and a transcendence").[65] The trace of
this visitation disjoins and *disturbs*, as can happen during
an unexpected, unhoped-for, or dreaded visit, expected or
awaited beyond all awaiting, like a messianic visit, perhaps,
but first of all because its past, the "passing" [*passée*] of the
guest, exceeds all anamnestic representation; it would never
belong to the memory of a past present:

> it is in the trace of the other that a face shines: what is pre-
> sented there is absolving itself from my life and visits me as al-
> ready ab-solute. Someone has already passed. His trace does
> not *signify* his past, as it does not *signify* his labor or his enjoy-
> ment in the world; it *is* a disturbance imprinting itself (we are
> tempted to say *engraving* itself) with an irrecusable gravity. . . .
>
> The God who passed is not the model of which the face
> would be an image. To be in the image of God does not
> mean to be an icon of God, but to find oneself in his trace.
> The revealed God of our Judeo-Christian spirituality main-
> tains all the infinity of his absence, which is in the personal
> "order" itself. He shows himself only by his trace, as is said in
> Exodus 33.[66]

Revelation, therefore, as *visitation*, from a place that
would be *common* to "our Judeo-Christian spirituality."

Are we to call this place Sinai, as this reference to chapter 33 of Exodus invites us to? In the words *visit* and *visitation*, is it really a question of *translating* this trace of the other into the vocabulary of hospitality, as we have seemed to assume? Must one not, on the contrary, refer the phenomenon and the possibility of hospitality back to this passing [*passée*] of visitation so as, first of all, to re-translate them? Does not hospitality *follow*, even if just by a second of secondariness, the unforeseeable and irresistible irruption of a visitation? And will not this inverse translation find its limit, the limit of the liminal itself, there where it is necessary to arrive, that is, at the place where, as past visitation, the trace of the other passes or has already passed the threshold, awaiting neither invitation nor hospitality nor welcome? This visit is not a response to an invitation; it exceeds every dialogical relation between host and guest. It *must*, from all time, have exceeded them. Its traumatizing effraction must have preceded what is so easily called hospitality—even, as disturbing and pervertible as they already appear, the laws of hospitality.

3. Finally, in the wake of this last reference, yet another question, that of the enigmatic relationship in Levinas's thought between an ethics and a politics of hospitality—or of the hostage. And precisely in the place where what is situated by the Sinai, or by the name of the Sinai, by the name "Sinai," belongs to several disjointed times, to several different occurrences that it is perhaps up to us to think *together*, without, however, synchronizing them or ordering them according to some grand chronology.

In a time that it is already difficult to hold as *one* and to bend to the homogeneity of a narrative without internal rupture, the name *Sinai* cannot but signify, obviously, at once the place where the Torah was given, the sacred annointing oil of messianity, the ark of the covenant, the tablets of the covenant written by the hand of God; but then also the tablets given by God after he retracts the evil with which he had threatened the stiff-necked people (first rupture or interruption), then the tablets broken (another interruption), then the tablets cut anew after God had in some sense again interrupted all theophany by forbidding, in the passing of his glory, the vision of his face in a face to face, then the place of the re-newed Covenant, then the veiling and unveiling of the face of Moses. So many interruptions *of self,* so many discontinuities in history, so many ruptures in the ordinary course of time, caesuras that nonetheless make up the very historicity of history.

But today Sinai is also, still in relation to the singular history of Israel, a name from modernity. Sinai, the Sinai: a metonymy for the border or frontier between Israel and the other nations, a front and a frontier between war and peace, a provocation to think the passage between the ethical, the messianic, eschatology, *and* the political, at a moment in the history of humanity and of the Nation-State when the persecution of all these hostages—the foreigner, the immigrant (with or without papers), the exile, the refugee, those without a country, or a State, the displaced person or population (so many distinctions that call for careful analysis)—seems, on every continent, open to a cruelty without precedent. Levinas never turned his eyes away from this violence and this distress, whether he spoke of it directly or not, in one way or another.

∼

Allow me here to grant some privilege to a passage that names at once *Sinai* and hospitality. It belongs to the talmudic readings that bear the title *In the Time of the Na-*

tions (*A l'heure des nations*, 1988). In the chapter "The Nations and the Presence of Israel," the title of a subchapter specifies "The Nations and Messianic Time." After having begun to comment on a psalm cited in the Tractate Pesahim, 118b, after having approached it with both rigor and inventiveness, with the difficult freedom that was his, Levinas throws out a question. He appears to leave it open and suspended, as if he were pretending to let it float in midair at the very moment he knows it to be held by so many threads, all barely visible and yet quite strong, following a discreet but nonetheless tenacious argument. The question in question hardly forms a sentence; it is a proposition without a verb, the tense or time of a few words followed by a question mark.

I would not want to overinterpret this curious concern, curious to question and to know, curious like a speculation, curious to see come, this at once timid and provocative hypothesis, secretly mischievous and jubilant, perhaps, in the discretion of its very ellipsis. It is contained in just a couple of words:

A recognition of the Torah before Sinai?

Let us venture a first translation: would there be a recognition of the law *before* the event, and thus *outside* the localizable event, before the singular, dated, and situated taking-place of the gift of the Torah to a people? Would there be such a *recognition*? Would it have been possible and thinkable? Before all revelation? A recognition of the Torah by the peoples or the nations for whom the name, the place, the event *Sinai* would mean nothing? Or nothing of what they mean for Israel or for what is named in the language of Israel? A recognition, in short, by some third? By some third following the play of substitution that would replace the unique with the unique?

The intrigue of this intriguing question, which, again, I do not want to take too far, even though the stakes are so high, is indeed a test of hospitality. A hospitality beyond all revelation. It is not a question, for Levinas, of calling into question the election of Israel, its unicity or its universal exemplarity, but, quite to the contrary, a question of recognizing a universal message for which it has responsibility before or independently of the place and the event of the gift of the law: human universality, humanitarian hospitality uprooted from a singularity of the event that would then become empirical, or at the most allegorical, perhaps only "political" in a very restricted sense of this term that will have to be clarified.

But the lesson to be drawn from this question or this interpretative speculation, the lesson of this lesson, would be yet another lesson for Israel to draw in its ethics—I dare not yet say its messianic politics—of hospitality. Of course, in this passage Israel does not primarily name the modern State, the one that bears, that gave itself or took for itself, the name Israel. But since the name "Israel" in this text does not name something else either, the historical and political space of these assigned names remains open.

To be more precise, let us try to reconstitute at least a part of the context, which would obviously call for a more patient reading. The psalm cited clearly describes a theater and some of the rites of hospitality:

> He also told him another thing: "Egypt will bring a gift to the Messiah in the future. He thought he should not accept it, coming from them, but the Holy One, Blessed be He, will say to the Messiah: 'Accept it from them; [after all] they *took in* [my emphasis, naturally] our children in Egypt.' Whereupon 'important persons will arrive from Egypt'" [Psalms 68: 32].[67]

These last words ("important persons will arrive from Egypt") cannot help but make us think of the way Levinas had, a few years earlier, hailed what he called "Sadat's grandeur and importance," the "exceptional transhistorical event" that his trip to Jerusalem was, a trip, he added, "that one neither makes nor is contemporaneous with twice in a lifetime."[68]

Now, after having cited this fragment, Levinas orients his interpretation toward the equivalence of *three concepts—fraternity, humanity, hospitality*—that determine an experience of the Torah and of the messianic times even *before* or outside of the Sinai, and even for the one who makes no claim "to the title of bearer or messenger of the Torah."

What announces itself here might be called a structural or *a priori* messianicity. Not an ahistorical messianicity, but one that belongs to a historicity without a particular and empirically determinable incarnation. Without revelation or without the dating of a given revelation. The hypothesis I am venturing here is obviously not Levinas's, at least not in this form, but it seeks to move in his direction—perhaps to cross his path once more. "At the heart of a chiasm," as he said one day.

These three concepts are, then:

1. *fraternity* (which is central to all of what follows in this talmudic reading and, in truth, in an explicit fashion, to Levinas's entire oeuvre; I have tried to explain elsewhere[69] my concerns about the prevalence of a certain figure of fraternity, and precisely in a certain relationship to femininity; I will not pause here to discuss this further, since this is really not my theme);

2. *humanity*, precisely as *fraternity* (the fraternity of the neighbor, a fundamental and omnipresent implication, a theme whose both Greek and biblical origin appears inef-

faceable, an equivalence that can also be found in Kant, among others, within a horizon that is more Christian than Judaic);

3. *hospitality*, a hospitality that comes to take on a much more radical value than it does in the Kant of *Toward Perpetual Peace* and of the cosmopolitical right to universal hospitality—yes, cosmo*political*, which is to say, only political and juridical, civil and state (always determined by citizenship).

But this third concept, *hospitality*, *asylum*, the *inn* (three words that appear within a page of one another to express sheltering or giving refuge in the open dwelling)—what Levinas calls the "place offered to the stranger"—is also the figural schema that gathers or collects these three concepts together, *fraternity*, *humanity*, *hospitality*: the welcome of the other or of the face as neighbor and as stranger, as neighbor *insofar as* he is a stranger, man and brother. The commentary that follows the citation of the tractate links these three concepts together according to the schema of transnational or universal (but let's not say *cosmopolitical*) hospitality:

This is the second teaching of Rabbi Yosé, transmitted to his son, Rabbi Ishmael, and communicated by the latter to Rabbi and proclaimed by Rav Kahana: The nations are determined to take part in the messianic age! [Levinas's exclamation point: a whole study would have to be devoted to Levinas's exclamation points, to the meaning, grammar, rhetoric, ethics, and pragmatics of this punctuation of address at the heart of a philosophical text. Like the word "marvel," which often precedes the exclamation point.] It is a recognition of the ultimate value of the human message borne by Judaism, a recognition reflected in or called for by the verses of Psalm 117. Has not the history of the nations already been in a sense that glorification of the Eternal in Israel, a participation in the history of Israel, which can be assessed by the degree to which their national solidarity is open to the other, the stranger? A recognition of the Torah before Sinai? The entire examination of this problem is tacitly related to a verse not quoted: Deuteronomy 23: 8. "Thou shalt not abhor an Edomite, for he is thy brother; thou shalt not abhor an Egyptian, because thou wast a stranger in his land." Fraternity (but what does it mean? Is it not, according to the Bible, a synonym of humanity?) and hospitality: are these not stronger than the horror a man may feel for the other who denies him in his alterity? Do they not already bring back a memory of the "Word of God"?[70]

What clearly seems suggested by these last words, "already . . . a memory of the 'Word of God,'" is a memory before memory, the memory of a word that will have taken place even before taking place, of a past event that is older than the past and more ancient than any memory ordered along the lines of an empirically determined string of presents, older than the Sinai, unless the allegorical anachrony in the name *Sinai* itself allows it to signify, through its own body, a foreign body, indeed, the body of the foreigner or stranger. This would designate precisely the experience *of* the stranger, where the truth of the messianic universe exceeds not only the determined place and moment, but also the identity, especially the national identity, of the bearer or messenger of the Torah, of the revealed Torah.

That is what the next lines of the commentary would seem to suggest:

> The Talmud will not enumerate all the nations—not even all those that appear in the Scriptures—and decide on their possible association with the messianic universe. The three nations or states or societies mentioned—Egypt, Cush and Rome—represent a typology of national life, in which, through the forms of existence that are pure history, there can be seen the inhuman or the human.

To explain this terrible alternative between the inhuman and the human, an alternative that already presupposes the face and peace, and thus hospitality, Levinas denounces the laying claim to being the historical messenger or the privileged—indeed the unique—interpreter of the Torah: "An allergy to or an aptitude for truth, without laying claim to the title of bearer or messenger of the Torah." The "without" of this proposition holds a great *analytical* power. The analysis seems to unbind or unseal the law from the event of its message, from the here-now of its revelation that bears the name *Sinai*, and the unbinding of this "without" seems to belong to the experience, evoked a moment ago, of a Torah *before* Sinai, of a "recognition of the Torah before Sinai," and if not a recognition without election (for the theme of election is everywhere at work in Levinas's analysis of ethical responsibility), at least an election whose assignation cannot be restricted to some particular place or moment and thus, perhaps, though one could not by definition ever be certain of this, to some particular people or nation. Let us never forget that election is inseparable from what always seems to contest it: substitution.

An irrecusable necessity, an irresistible force, a force that is nonetheless made vulnerable by a certain weakness: this *thinking of* substitution leads us toward a logic that is hardly thinkable, almost unsayable, that of the possible-impossible, the iterability and replaceability of the unique in the very experience of unicity as such.[71]

IV

By means of discreet though transparent allusions, Levinas oriented our gazes toward what is happening today, not only in Israel but in Europe and in France, in Africa,

America, and Asia, since at least the time of the First
World War and since what Hannah Arendt called *The
Decline of the Nation State*: everywhere that refugees of
every kind, immigrants with or without citizenship, exiled
or forced from their homes, whether with or without papers, from the heart of Nazi Europe to the former Yugoslavia, from the Middle East to Rwanda, from Zaire all
the way to California, from the Church of St. Bernard to
the thirteenth arrondissement in Paris, Cambodians, Arme-
nians, Palestinians, Algerians, and so many others call for
a change in the socio- and geo-political space—a juridico-
political mutation, though, before this, assuming that this
limit still has any pertinence, an ethical conversion.

Emmanuel Levinas speaks—indeed, already long ago
began to speak—of this distress and this call. The miracle
of the trace that allows us to read him today and to hear
his voice resonate and thus have meaning for us is taking
place once again. It is intensified, one might say, by the
crimes against hospitality endured by the guests [*hôtes*]
and hostages of our time, incarcerated or deported day after day, from concentration camp to detention camp,
from border to border, close to us or far away. (Yes, crimes
against hospitality, to be distinguished from an "offense
of hospitality [*délit d'hospitalité*]," as today it is once
again being called in French law, in the spirit of the decrees and ordinances of 1938 and 1945 that would pun-
ish—and even imprison—anyone taking in a foreigner in
an illegal situation.)

Levinas speaks to us in this way of the gift of the inn, of
shelter and asylum: "God requires him to accept the gift,
reminding him of the asylum offered Israel by the country of Egypt. Asylum that will become a place of slav-
ery—but first a place offered to the stranger. Already a
song of glory to the God of Israel!"[72] The hospitality of-

fered would thus itself signify a belonging to the messianic order.

Just as he recalled a memory of the immemorial, so Levinas denounces, in passing, a certain forgetting of the law. It is once again the moment of welcoming, for *welcoming* is the word used to describe the divine decision:

> A decision by the Eternal to welcome Egypt's homage. [The Eternal is the *hôte* (the host) welcoming the *hôte* (the guest), who pays him homage in a classic scene of hospitality.] The Bible renders that foreseeable in Deuteronomy 23: 8, a verse the Messiah himself, despite his justice, must have forgotten. One belongs to the messianic order when one has been able to admit others among one's own. That a people should accept those who come and settle among them—even though they are foreigners with their own customs and clothes, their own way of speaking, their own smell—that a people should give them an *akhsaniah*, such as a place at the inn, and the wherewithal to breathe and to live—is a song to the glory of the God of Israel.[73]

That a people, as a people, "should accept those who come and settle among them—even though they are foreigners," would be the proof [*gage*] of a popular and public commitment [*engagement*], a political *res publica* that cannot be reduced to a sort of "tolerance," unless this tolerance requires the affirmation of a "love" without measure. Levinas specifies immediately thereafter that this duty of hospitality is not only essential to a "Jewish thought" of the relationships between Israel and the nations. It opens the way to the humanity of the human in general. There is here, then, a daunting logic of election and exemplarity operating between the assignation of a singular responsibility and human universality—today one might even say *humanitarian* universality insofar as it would at least try, despite all the difficulties and ambiguities, to remain, in the form, for example, of a non-governmental organization, beyond Nation-States and their politics.

The rest of this passage might today be illustrated, if this word were not indecent, by all the examples on earth. For the question of borders is no doubt the question of Israel, but the question also goes beyond the border lines of what is called or what calls itself Israel, in the biblical sense and in the sense of the modern state. "To shelter the other in one's own land or home, to tolerate the presence of the landless and homeless on the 'ancestral soil,' so jealously, so meanly loved—is that the criterion of humanness? Unquestionably so."[74]

This text dates from the 1980's. One would have to read it together with many others that also turn around the question of the State and the Nation, beginning with the one to which we alluded earlier, which hails "Sadat's grandeur and [transhistorical] importance." One would also have to go back to the distant premises of this discourse in *Totality and Infinity* and *Otherwise than Being*. Let us recall at least this sign in a few words: the "Talmudic Readings and Lectures" gathered together in 1982 at the end of *Beyond the Verse* (under the title—in the plural—"Zionisms"), "The State of Caesar and the State of David," 1971, and then "Politics After!," 1979, multiply propositions that have a form, and I emphasize *form*, that is deliberately contradictory, aporetic, indeed dialectical (in the sense of a transcendental dialectic)—proportions at once intra-political and transpolitical, at once *for and against* the "state principle," against what *Totality and Infinity* had already called the "tyranny of the State" (according to an anti-Hegelian move in the style, at least, of Rosenzweig), against the State of Caesar, which, "despite its participation in the pure essence of the State, is also the place of corruption *par excellence* and, perhaps, the ultimate refuge of idolatry";[75] against the State and yet leaving to what Levinas calls the "beyond of the State" or the "going beyond of the State" an opening toward the "culmination of the State of David" in the messianic State, a going beyond of the State toward a "world to come."[76] The *going beyond* of one State (that of Caesar), the *culmination* of another (that of David), both of which might appear utopic or premature, as Levinas recognizes, but which point to the very opening of the political toward its future, if it has one. (If one took it as a rule to speak of "politics" as soon as the word "State" appears, in a more or less rigorous translation of *Polis*, then one would have to ask if this rule applies in the expression "State of David," or if the alternative between the State of Caesar and the State of David is an alternative between a politics and a beyond of the political, or an alternative between two politics, or, finally, *an* alternative among *others*, where one could not exclude the hypothesis of a State that would be neither Caesar's nor David's, neither Rome nor Israel nor Athens. We will close these parenthetical remarks, but not before insisting on the fact that Levinas does not hesitate to speak of a "messianic politics," which is to be distinguished from what we understand by politics in the tradition—in the, let's say, Greek or post-Hellenic tradition—that dominates Western politology. When he says "beyond politics," "politics" always means this non-messianic politics of the State, which is transgressed toward its beyond by that which nonetheless remains a politics, still a politics, but a messianic politics. It is true that the border line, the frontier, the semantic identity of all these words here begins to tremble, and that is the most undeniable effect of this writing, the very thrust of this thought. "The messianic City," says Levinas, "is not beyond politics," and he adds, "the City in its simplest sense is never this side of the religious."[77]

Against this backdrop, Levinas ventures a hypothesis that could be considered rather audacious, in more than one way: on the one hand, the distinction between the earthly City and the City of God, between the political order and the spiritual one, would not have in pre- or post-Christian Judaism the "clear-cut character" it has in Christianity; on the other hand, it is, paradoxically, because of what Levinas does not hesitate to call, precisely because of this strict separation, Christianity's "political indifference," that Christianity has "so often become a State religion."[78] The political indifference elicits a taste for power for the sake of power, of whatever kind and at whatever cost. It would condone the uncontrolled authoritarianism and dogmatism of the Church whenever it dominates the State. This thesis or hypothesis is appealing, perhaps profound, certainly very rich, but also rather confidently advanced, if I may say so, and rather quickly asserted, not only with regard to the link between political indifference and State religion but especially with regard to the presumed absence of State religion outside of a Christian space: in Islamic lands (Levinas makes no mention of this), but also in the land of Israel, although the expression "State religion" is fraught with difficulties in this case, too elusive for either strictly affirming or denying (as Levinas is sometimes tempted to do)[79] the existence of a State religion in Israel.

The deliberately aporetic, paradoxical, or undecidable form of these statements on the political will later find one of its titles in the lesson of December 5, 1988, included this past year, after the death of Emmanuel Levinas, in *Nouvelles lectures talmudiques*. In this title, the political seems to defy any topological simplicity: it is "Beyond the State in the State." *Beyond-in*: transcendence in immanence, *beyond* the political, but *in* the political. Inclusion opened onto the transcendence that it bears, incorporation of a door [*porte*] that bears [*porte*] and opens onto the beyond of the walls and partitions framing it. At the risk of causing the identity of the place as well as the stability of the concept to implode. This lesson assigns to the transcendence included the space of a "messianic politics," an "acceptable political order that can come to the human only from the Torah, from its justice, its judges and its master savants."[80]

Just before this, Levinas devotes some time to a Midrash reading that takes the liberty of isolating the first few words of a verse: "Here's the Torah: the man who dies."[81] (We will have to speak again about death, the moment of the "without response," and about the Torah, about the *à-Dieu* and the "without response," and, finally, about a Torah whose hospitality would also protect the dead from death.) The "democratic State," the only State open to perfectibility, has just been defined as the only "exception to the tyrannical rule of political power."[82] In the course of these reflections, there arises the question of what comes to pass, of who comes or what comes to pass, when Alexander comes into a city of women, only women, who disarm him with their questions. Alexander ends by concluding (a teaching that calls for serious reflection when one is interested in a politics that would take into account the voices of women, at home and outside the home): "I, Alexander of Macedonia, was a fool before having come into this country of women in Africa and before having taken their advice."[83]

In *Beyond the Verse*, a subchapter of "The State of Caesar and the State of David" entitled "Towards a Monotheistic Politics" follows one entitled "Beyond the State,"

which follows yet another entitled "Yes to the State."
Now, one cannot overstate the importance of the discursive modalities that here multiply question marks, conditionals, and what might be called epochal clauses. These precautions reflect rhetorical, indeed political, caution less than they constitute ways of respecting or greeting what remains to come—a future of which we know nothing. What comes will never belong to the order of knowledge or of fore-knowledge.

In the conclusion of "Towards a Monotheistic Politics," for example, this epochal reserve is marked in words that I am about to emphasize (*"commitment," "but"*): "Israel had become incapable of thinking a politics which would bring to perfection its monotheistic message. Henceforth, the *commitment* [*engagement*] has been made. Since 1948. *But* everything has only just begun."

There is a date here: "since 1948." It recalls an event, the foundation of a State that *commits itself* to being *not only* what it also is, in fact and by law—that is, a State like any other. While neither approving nor disapproving of the juridical *fact*, the foundation of the modern State of Israel, consecrated through law by a majority of states in the international community, Levinas sees in this only a "commitment." A huge commitment, *but* only a commitment. And since this political history, he says, "has only just begun," the betrayal of the commitment, its breach or perjury, is always possible for what can become a State like any other, indeed sometimes and in certain respects, some would say, worse than many others, than certain others. Everything remains suspended, all statements under surveillance, as we will hear, by the cautious vigilance of a conditional. The commitment should go "beyond," in Levinas's word—beyond the political, beyond a strictly "political" problem or solution in the national or familial arena.

Henceforth, the *commitment* has been made. Since 1948. *But* everything has only just begun. Israel is no less isolated in its struggle to complete its extraordinary task than was Abraham, who began it four thousand years ago. [This passing remark on the isolation of Israel can be disputed, indeed it is to my mind disputable, but since it is not strictly essential or necessary to the argumentative structure that interests me here, I will simply leave the question open.] But this return to the land of our ancestors—*beyond* solving any specific problems, whether national or familial—*would* thus mark one of the greatest events of internal history and, indeed, of all History.[84]

These are the final words of "The State of Caesar and the State of David." They speak of an unconditional *commitment*, to be sure, but, like the description of the political event, the interpretation of its future remains couched in the conditional. (We will return to this. We will also return, in conclusion, to the parenthetical remark with which I allowed myself to draw off my own parenthetical remark, thereby detaching it from the argumentative structure that we have privileged and are trying to follow here.)

V

"Politics After!": under this title, a cautious interpretation of Zionism attempts to distinguish, rightly or wrongly, between two major phases. But is it a question of phases? A question of a historical sequence? Or is it, on the contrary, a question of two worlds? Of two competing and irreconcilable figures? Of two Zionisms that forever fight over the same time?

Levinas clearly privileges diachrony: there would be first of all a realist Zionism, more *political* and, perhaps, "inadequate to the prophetic ideal." Perhaps more inclined to the current nationalism, this political Zionism would explain, in pre-Hitlerian Europe and sometimes still today, a reticence on the part of certain Jews who align themselves with a "universalist finality."[85] A second Zionism would be more open to the eschatological vision of a holy history, or else, and indeed through this—a politics beyond the political—to what Levinas calls a "political invention."[86]

Whether or not one endorses any of these analyses of the actual situation of the State of Israel in its political visibility (and I must admit that I do not always do so), the concern here is incontestable: *on the one hand*, to interpret the Zionist *commitment*, the promise, the sworn faith and not the Zionist *fact*, as a movement that carries the political *beyond* the political, and thus is caught between the political and its other; and, *on the other hand*, to think a peace that would not be purely political.

Assuming that these two distinctions make any sense and can be used (*concesso non dato*), in neither case does the beyond of the political, the beyond of the *purely* political, gesture toward the non-political. It announces another politics, messianic politics, that of the State of David as opposed to the State of Caesar, that is, as opposed to the classical and hegemonic tradition of the State as it is found in what we must try to identify, with all requisite precautions, as *our* politology, the discourse of the Greco-Roman philosophical tradition on the political, the City, the State, war and peace. This assumes, of course, that short of identifying such a thing as Western politology with itself—something we must keep from doing, especially under the imperial rather than democratic figure of the State of Caesar—one can nonetheless recognize a dominant tendency, one that is closer to Caesar than to David and that would make democracy itself imperialist in vocation. So many hypotheses, and the question of what is to be understood by this word "political," and whether the borders of this concept today resist analysis, remains open. We cannot directly approach this question here. We would need a guiding thread or touchstone in the context that concerns us. The idea of peace, for example, in its obvious and continuously reaffirmed affinity with hospitality. Is peace something political? In what sense? Under what conditions? How are we to read Levinas's "suggestion," in his words, "that peace is a concept that goes beyond purely political thought"?[87]

Levinas makes a "suggestion," just a suggestion, at once confident and uneasy. He does not assert that peace *is* a *non-political concept*, but suggests that this concept *perhaps exceeds* the political.

What does this imply? A difficult division or partition: in sum, without being at peace with itself, such a concept of peace retains a political *part*, it *participates* in the political, even if another part of it goes beyond a certain concept of the political. The concept exceeds itself, goes beyond its own borders, which amounts to saying that it interrupts itself or deconstructs itself so as to form a sort of enclave inside and outside of itself: "beyond in," once again, the political interiorization of ethical or messianic transcendence. (And let us note in passing that each time this interruption of self takes place or is produced [we have been following a few examples of this for some time now], each time this delimitation of self, which might also pass for an excess or transcendence of self, is produced, each time this topological enclave affects a concept, a process of deconstruction is in progress, which is no longer a teleological process or even a simple event in the course of history). As if the word "suggestion" did not suffice to signal a vigilant circumspection, Levinas goes on to specify that,

in part, "peace is a concept that goes beyond" not the political, but "*purely* political thought." This insistence bears
everything; it is necessary to insist upon purity.

Here, then, is a "concept," peace, the thought of which
would go beyond any thought that would wish to remain
purely political. A "purely political thought" would be inadequate to this concept. To think this concept of peace,
it would be necessary to leave not the order of the political, but the order of what Levinas calls the "purely political." To know what the political is, we would need to
know what the "purely political" is. A fiction for which
Levinas in fact, in another place, excludes the possibility
of ever taking shape, of ever being embodied, of ever taking on a real body, since, as we have heard, "the City in its
simplest sense is never this side of the religious." Indeed,
he speaks of this not purely political peace in the context
of inventing the political, of a "political invention," more
precisely, of "creating on its land [the land of the State of
Israel] the concrete conditions for political invention."[88]

Has this *political invention* in Israel ever come to pass?
Ever come to pass in Israel? This is perhaps not the place
to pose this question, certainly not to answer it; we would
not have the time, and indeed not just the time, for all the
requisite analyses—but does one have the right here to silence the anxiety of such an interrogation, before these
words of Levinas, and in the spirit that inspires them?
Would such a silence be worthy of the responsibilities that
we have been assigned? First of all, before Emmanuel Levinas himself? I am among those who await this "political
invention" in Israel, among those who call for it in hope,
today more than ever because of the despair that recent
events, to mention only them, have not attenuated (for
example, though these are just examples from yesterday
and today, the renewed support of colonial "settlements"

or the decision by the supreme Court authorizing torture, and, more generally, all the initiatives that suspend, derail, or interrupt what continues to be called, in this manner of speaking, the "peace process").

In any case, even if this suggestion of Levinas remains, in the end, enigmatic, it gestures toward a peace that is *neither* purely political, in the traditional sense of this term, *nor* simply apolitical. It belongs to a context where the reaffirmation of ethics, the subjectivity of the host as the subjectivity of the hostage, broaches the passage from the political toward the beyond of the political or toward the "already non-political." Where are the borders between the "already" and the "not yet"? Between politics and the non-political? A few pages earlier Levinas writes:

> From the outset, self-assertion is responsibility for everyone. *Political and already non-political.* Epic and Passion. Irrepressible energy and extreme vulnerability. After the realism of its political formulations at the beginning, Zionism is finally revealing itself, on the scale of substantial Judaism, as a great ambition of the Spirit.[89]

What does "already" mean in the expression "and already non-political"? How might this "and already non-" eat into what it still is, namely, "political"? Or how might it let itself be eaten into by what it already no longer is, that is, "political," by what is still eating into it? What does "political" mean when one appeals to a peace whose "concept . . . goes beyond purely political thought"?

These words belong to a text entitled "Politics After!," published in 1979 in *Les temps modernes* and reprinted in 1982 in *L'au-delà du verset* [later translated as *Beyond the Verse*]. Followed by an exclamation point, the title "Politics After!" seems clear: let politics come after, in second place! The primordial or final injunction, what is most urgent, would not be first of all political, purely political. Politics or the political should follow, come "after"; it must be subordinated—whether in logical consequence or chronological sequence—to an injunction that transcends the political order. As far as the political order is concerned, we will see afterwards, it will come later; politics will follow, like day-to-day operations: "Politics After!"

"We are following in the wake of Sadat's trip to Jerusalem, an act of quasi-messianic audacity, hailed as this "exceptional transhistorical event that one neither makes nor is contemporaneous with twice in a lifetime. . . . All the impossible becoming possible."[90]

One might be tempted to transpose or reverse things today. This expression—"all the impossible becoming possible"—does not sound like a merely fortuitous echo of the "possibility of the impossible" of which "Substitution" speaks with regard to an absolute passivity, which is not that of death (in the Heideggerian sense of the possibility of the impossible), but the condition of the hostage, of the "I am a hostage" and of the "infinite responsibility" that obligates me toward the neighbor as the third, a "passivity that is not only the possibility of death in being, the possibility of impossibility, but an impossibility that is prior to this possibility, the impossibility of slipping away." Our responsibility, in short, before or prior to death, standing before death, before the dead, beyond death. Here, now, the impossible has become possible. Since the coming of Sadat to Jerusalem. Did not Sadat in fact understand

> the opportunities opened up through friendship with Israel—or simply through already recognizing its existence and entering into talks—and all the prophetic promises that are hidden behind the Zionist claim to historical rights and its contortions under the political yoke? All injustices, capable of being put right.

Levinas continues:

All the impossible becoming possible. Which less lofty minds among Sadat's enemies in the Near East, or his friends in our proud West, have never sensed, plunged as they are in their political bookkeeping. "A State like any other" and a lot of eloquence? Oh really! So there would be no alternative between recourse to unscrupulous methods whose model is furnished by *Realpolitik* and the irritating rhetoric of a careless idealism, lost in utopian dreams but crumbling into dust on contact with reality or turning into a dangerous, impudent and facile frenzy which professes to be taking up the prophetic discourse? Beyond the State of Israel's concern to provide a refuge for men without a homeland and its sometimes surprising, sometimes uncertain achievements, has it not, above all, been a question of creating on its land the concrete conditions for political invention? That is the ultimate culmination of Zionism, and thereby probably one of the great events in human history. For two thousand years the Jewish people was only the object of history, in a state of political innocence which it owed to its role as victim. That role is not enough for its vocation. But since 1948 this people has been surrounded by enemies and is still being called into question [this "being-in-question" defines, we recall, the subjectivity or ipseity of the hostage: persecution, obsession, or obsidionality, responsibility for all], yet engaged too in real events, in order to think—and to make and remake—a State which will have to incarnate the prophetic moral code and the idea of its peace. That this idea has already managed to be handed down and caught in full flight, as it were, is the wonder of wonders. As we have already said, Sadat's trip has opened up the unique path for peace in the Near East, if this peace is to be possible at all. For what is 'politically' weak about it is probably the expression both of its audacity and, ultimately, of its strength. It is also, perhaps, what it brings, for everyone everywhere, to the very idea of peace: the suggestion that peace is a concept which goes beyond purely political thought.[91]

What is peace? What are we saying when we say "peace"? What does it mean "to be at peace with"—to be at peace with someone else, a group, a State, a nation, oneself as another? In each of these cases, one can be at peace only with some other. So long as what is other as other will not have been in some way "welcomed" in epiphany, in the withdrawal or visitation of its face, it would make no sense to speak of peace. With the same, one is never at peace.

Even if this axiom appears impoverished and abstract, it is not so easy to think through. What is the semantic kernel, if there is one and if it has a unity, of this little word *paix* ["peace"]? Is there such a semantic kernel? In other words, is there a concept of peace? One that would be *one*, indestructible in its identity? Or must we invent another relation to this concept, as perhaps to any concept, to the non-dialectical enclosure of its own transcendence, its "beyond-in"?

Just as we should have asked what we mean when we say "to welcome" or "to receive"—and all of Levinas's thought is, wants to be, and presents itself as a teaching (in the sense of magisterial height that he gives to this word, and that he confers upon it in a magisterial way), a teaching on the subject of what "to welcome" or "to receive" *should* mean—so we *should* ask what the word "peace" can and *should* mean, as opposed to war *or not*.

As opposed to war and thus to hostility *or not*, since this opposition cannot simply be assumed. To war or to hostilities, to hostility itself, that is to say, to a declared hostility that is also, it is often believed, the contrary of hospitality. Now if war and declared hostility were the same thing, and if they were the opposite of peace, then one would also have to say that peace and the hospitality of welcoming also form a pair, an inseparable pair, a correlation in which one of them, peace, is on a par with the other, hospitality, and vice versa.

We must perhaps problematize, disturb, trouble, or suspect all these pairs of concepts, which are assumed to be synonymous, co-implicated, or symmetrically opposable. It is not certain that "war," "hostility," and "conflict" are the same thing. (Kant, for example, distinguishes between war and conflict.) It is also not certain that hospitality and peace are synonyms. One can imagine a political peace between two States where no hospitality would be offered to the citizens of the other State, or where strict conditions would be placed on any hospitality. In fact, this is what most often happens. War and peace are also too often thought to form a symmetrical pair of opposed concepts. But give to one or the other of these two concepts a value or position of originarity, and the symmetry is broken.

If one thinks, like Kant, that everything in nature begins with war, then at least two consequences follow. First, peace is no longer a natural phenomenon, one that is symmetrical and simply opposable to war; it is a phenomenon of another order, of a non-natural nature, of an institutional (and thus politico-juridical) nature. Second, peace is not simply the cessation of hostilities, an abstention from making war or an armistice; it must be instituted as perpetual peace, as the promise of eternal peace. Eternity is then neither a utopia, nor a hollow word, nor some external or supplementary predicate to be attached to the concept of peace. The concept implies, in itself, analytically, in its own necessity, that peace is eternal. The thought of eternity is indestructible in the very concept of peace, and thus in the concept of hospitality, if this can be thought. The Kantian argument is well known: if I make peace with the thought in the back of my mind of reopening hostilities, of returning to war, or of agreeing only to an armistice, if I even think that one day, more or less in spite of myself, I should let myself be won over by the hypothesis of another war, this would not be peace. There may then, never be any peace, one might say, but if there were, it would have to be eternal and, as an instituted, juridico-political peace, not natural.

Some might conclude from this that there never is and never will be such a peace. A purely political peace might always not take place in conditions adequate to its concept. Henceforth, this eternal peace, purely political as it is, is not political, or the political is never adequate to its concept. Which, in spite of all the differences to which we must be attentive, would bring Kant closer to Levinas when, in "Politics After!," the latter takes note of this concept of the political, of its inadequation to itself or to its infinite idea, and of the consequences that Kant is forced to draw from it in his "Third Definitive Article for a Perpetual Peace": "The Law of World Citizenship Shall Be Limited to Conditions of Universal Hospitality." This generous article is in fact limited by a great number of conditions: universal hospitality is here only juridical and political; it grants only the right of temporary sojourn and not the right of residence; it concerns only the citizens of States; and, in spite of its institutional character, it is founded on a natural right, the common possession of the round and finite surface of the earth, across which humans cannot spread ad infinitum. The realization of this natural right, and thus of universal hospitality, is referred to a cosmopolitical constitution that the human species can only approach indefinitely.

But for all these reasons, which indefinitely suspend and condition the immediate, infinite, and unconditional welcoming of the other, Levinas always prefers, and I would want to say this without any play on words, *peace*

now, and he prefers universality to cosmopolitanism. To
my knowledge, Levinas never uses the word "cosmopolitanism" or adopts it as his own. I can imagine at least two
reasons for this: first, because this sort of political thought
refers pure hospitality, and thus peace, to an indefinite
progress; second, because of the well-known ideological
connotations with which modern anti-Semitism saddled
the great tradition of a cosmopolitanism passed down
from Stoicism or Pauline Christianity to the Enlightenment and to Kant.

Whereas for Kant the institution of an eternal peace, of
a cosmopolitical law, and of a universal hospitality, retains
the trace of a natural hostility, whether present or threatening, real or virtual, for Levinas the contrary would be
so: war itself retains the testimonial trace of a pacific welcoming of the face. In the beginning of section 2 of *Perpetual Peace*, Kant declares war to be *natural*:

> The state of peace among men living side by side is not the
> natural state (*status naturalis*) [*Naturzustand*]: the natural
> state is one of war [*Zustand des Krieges*]. This does not always
> mean open hostilities [literally: even if there is no outbreak
> of enmity, of hostility: *wenngleich nicht immer ein Ausbruch
> der Feindseligkeiten*], but at least an unceasing threat [*Bedro-
> hung*] of war.[92]

For Kant, and this must be taken seriously, a threat of
war, a simple pressure—whether symbolic, diplomatic, or
economic—is enough to interrupt the peace. Potential or
virtual hostility remains incompatible with peace. This
goes very far, and penetrates very deeply, rendering every
virtual allergy, whether unconscious or radically forbidden, contradictory to peace. The first appearance of any
threat would be incompatible with peace, the immanence
and not just the imminence of a negativity in the experi-

ence of peace. Only this allows Kant to conclude that there is no natural peace, and that, as he says immediately thereafter, the state of peace must thus be *"instituted"* (founded, *gestiftet*).

But as soon as peace is instituted, politically deliberated, juridically constructed, does it not indefinitely and inevitably retain within it a trace of the violent nature with which it is supposed to break, the nature it is supposed to interrupt, interdict, or repress? Kant does not say this, but can it not be thought, either with or against him, that an institutional peace is at once pure and impure? As an eternal promise, it must retain, according to a logic that I tried elsewhere to formalize,[93] the trace of a threat, of what threatens it and of what threatens in it, thus contaminating the promise by a threat, according to a collusion that is deemed, particularly by the theoreticians of the promise as *speech act*, inacceptable, inadmissible, and contrary to the very essence of the promise. Kant continues:

> A state of peace, therefore, must be *instituted* [*es muss also gestiftet werden*], for in order to be secured against hostility it is not sufficient that hostilities simply be not committed; and, unless this security is pledged to each by his neighbor (a thing that can occur only in a civic state [*in einem gesetzlichen Zustande*]), each may treat his neighbor, from whom he demands this security, as an enemy.

If everything begins, as nature and in nature, with a real or virtual war, there is no longer a symmetrical opposition between war and peace, that is, between war and perpetual peace. Hospitality, which would retain the trace of a possible war, can then only be conditional, juridical, political. A Nation-State, indeed a community of Nation-States, can only condition peace, just as it can only limit hospitality, refuge, or asylum. And the first—indeed the only—concern of Kant is to define limitations and conditions. We know this only too well: never will a Nation-State as such, regardless of its form of government, and even if it is democratic, its majority on the right or the left, open itself up to an unconditional hospitality or to a right of asylum without restriction. It would never be "realistic" to expect or demand this of a Nation-State as such. The Nation-State will always want to "control the flow of immigration."

Now, could it not be said, inversely, that for Levinas everything begins with peace? Although this peace is *neither natural* (since, and this is not fortuitous, there is no concept of nature or reference to a state of nature in Levinas, it seems to me, and this is of the utmost importance: before nature, before the originarity of the archē, there is what works always to interrupt it, the pre-original anachrony of an-archy), *nor simply institutional or juridico-political*, everything seems "to begin," in a precisely an-archic and anachronic fashion, by the welcoming of the face of the other in hospitality, which is also to say, by its immediate and quasi-immanent interruption in the illeity of the third.

But the rupture of this symmetry, which seems to be the inverse of that described by Kant, has its own equivocal consequences. It suggests that war, hostility, even murder, *still* presuppose and thus *always* manifest this originary welcoming that is openness to the face: before and after Sinai. One can make war only against a face; one can kill, or give oneself the prohibition not to kill, only where the epiphany of the face has taken place, even if one rejects, forgets, or denies it in an allergic reaction. We know that, for Levinas, the prohibition against killing, the "Thou shalt not kill," in which, as he says, "The entire Torah" is gathered,[94] and which "the face of the other signifies," is the very origin of ethics.

Whereas for Kant the institution of peace could not but retain the trace of a warlike state of nature, in Levinas the inverse is the case, since allergy, the rejection of the other, even war, appear in a space marked by the epiphany of the face, where "the subject is a host" and a "hostage," where consciousness of . . . , or intentional subjectivity, as responsible, traumatized, obsessed, and persecuted, first offers the hospitality that it is. When Levinas affirms that the essence of language is goodness, or that "the essence of language is friendship and hospitality," he clearly intends to mark an interruption: an interruption of both symmetry and dialectic. He breaks with both Kant and Hegel, with both a juridico-cosmopolitanism that, in spite of its claims to the contrary, could never succeed in interrupting an armed peace, peace as armistice, and with the laborious process—the work—of the negative, "with a peace process" that would still organize war by other means when it does not make of it a condition of consciousness, of "objective morality" (*Sittlichkeit*) and of politics—the very thing that the dialectic of Carl Schmitt, for example, still credited to Hegel.[95] For Levinas, peace is not a process of the negative, the result of a dialectical treaty between the same and the other: "The other is not the negation of the same, as Hegel would like to say. The fundamental fact of the ontological scission into same and other is a non-allergic relation of the same with the other."

These are the final pages of *Totality and Infinity*. They declare peace, peace now, before and beyond any peace process, even before any "peace now movement."[96]

Where might we find a rule or mediating schema between this pre-originary hospitality or this peace without process and, on the other side, politics, the politics of modern States (whether existing or in the process of being constituted), for example, since this is only an example, the politics underway in the "peace process" between Israel and Palestine? All the rhetorics and all the strategies that claim to refer to this today do so in the name of and with a view to "politics" that are not only different but apparently antagonistic and incompatible.

The final pages of *Totality and Infinity* return to the propositions that, in the chapter entitled "The Dwelling," refer to language in terms of non-violence, peace, and hospitality. Levinas there speaks of what "is produced in language," namely, "the positive deployment of this *pacific* [my emphasis] relation with the other, without any border or negativity." Twice in a few lines, the word "hospitality" is identified with recollection in the home, but with *recollection* [*recueillement*] as *welcome* [*accueil*]: "Recollection in a home open to the Other—hospitality—is the concrete and initial fact of human recollection and separation; it coincides with the Desire for the Other absolutely transcendent."[97]

The at-home-with-oneself of the dwelling does not imply a closing off, but rather the place of Desire toward the transcendence of the other. The separation marked here is the condition of both the welcome and the hospitality offered to the other. There would be neither welcome nor hospitality without this radical alterity, which itself presupposes separation. The social bond is a certain experience of the unbinding without which no respiration, no spiritual inspiration, would be possible. Recollection, indeed being-together itself, presupposes infinite separation. The at-home-with-oneself would thus no longer be a sort of nature or rootedness but a response to a wandering, to the phenomenon of wandering it brings to a halt.

This axiom also holds for the space of the nation. The ground or the territory has nothing natural about it, nothing of a root, even if it is sacred, nothing of a possession

for the national occupant. The earth gives hospitality before all else, a hospitality already offered to the initial occupant, a temporary hospitality granted to the *hôte*, even
if he remains the master of the place. He thus comes to be
received in "his" own home. Right there in the middle of
Totality and Infinity, the "home," the familial home, "the
dwelling" in which the figure of woman plays the essential
role of the absolute welcomer, turns out to be a *chosen,
elected,* or rather *allotted* home, a home that is entrusted,
assigned by the choice of an election, and so not at all a
natural place.

> The chosen home [Levinas says, just after having spoken of
> hospitality as the Desire for the Other absolutely transcen-
> dent] is the very opposite of a root. It indicates a disengage-
> ment, a wandering which has made it possible, which is not
> a *less* with respect to installation, but the surplus of the rela-
> tionship with the Other, metaphysics.[98]

In the final pages of *Totality and Infinity*, we find the
same themes of hospitable peace and uprooted wandering. Bypassing the political in the usual sense of the term,
the same logic opens a wholly other space: before, beyond,
outside the State. But one must wonder why it now cen-
ters this "situation," no longer on the femininity of welcoming, but on paternal fecundity, on what Levinas calls,
and this would be another large question, yet another
marvel, the "marvel of the family." This marvel con-
cretizes "the infinite time of fecundity"—a non-biological
fecundity, of course—"the instant of eroticism and the infinity of paternity."[99]

Though they are placed under the sign of a declared
peace and hospitality ("Metaphysics, or the relation to the
other, is accomplished as service and as hospitality"),[100]
the "Conclusions" of *Totality and Infinity* no longer relate

this "hospitable welcome" to "the feminine being" ("the hospitable welcome par excellence," "the welcoming one par excellence," "welcoming in itself" of "The Dwelling") but to paternal fecundity, which opens up "an infinite and discontinuous time,"[101] and which, as we recalled above, has an essential, if not exclusive, relation with the son, with each son insofar as he is a "unique son," an "only son" [*fils unique*], a "chosen son." Where the feminine being seemed to be the figure of "the welcoming one par excellence," the father now becomes the infinite host or the host of the infinite.

It is a question of opposing to the State what is here inscribed on only one side of sexual difference, under the sole law of paternity, namely, the "infinite time of fecundity," and not the "egoist protestation of subjectivity." With this insistent gesture, with this protestation against subjective protestation, Levinas seems to want to distance himself from two thinkers who are very close to him: from both a certain Kierkegaard (whose interpretation of the "sacrifice" of Isaac and of the paternal figure of Abraham he contests elsewhere) and a certain Rosenzweig. Before both of them, he feigns to be tempted for a moment by the Hegelian argument that would favor the universality of the State. He feigns this, but only so as to let it be heard without feigning that one must not close oneself up in the subjective finitude of the *ego*—something from which "fecundity," precisely, the infinite time of the father-son relation, would protect us:

> Against this egoist protestation of the subjectivity, against this protestation in the first person, the universalism of Hegelian reality will perhaps prevail. . . . The I is conserved then in goodness, without its resistance to system manifesting itself as the egoist cry of the subjectivity, still concerned for happiness or salvation, as in Kierkegaard.[102]

An apparent paradox: anarchy, true anarchy, must be paternal—as the only effective protestation against the "tyranny of the State." Pre-originary hospitality, anarchic goodness, infinite fecundity, and paternity might still give way to allergy. This happens almost all the time and it entails forgetting, denying, or repressing what comes before the origin, according to the common experience of history. This negativity of repression would always remain, according to Levinas, secondary—even if it were an originary repression, as is said in the psychoanalytical code of which Levinas is wary. In its originary secondariness, it would still attest, as if in spite of itself, to the very thing it forgets, denies, or represses, so that inhospitality, allergy, war, etc. would still come to *bear witness* to the fact that everything begins with their contrary, that is, with hospitality.

Henceforth, a hierarchizing dissymmetry remains (one that is apparently the inverse of Kant's). War or allergy, the inhospitable rejection, is still derived from hospitality. Hostility manifests hospitality; it remains in spite of itself a phenomenon of hospitality, with the frightful consequence that war might always be interpreted as the continuation of peace by other means, or at least as the non-interruption of peace or hospitality. Hence this great messianic discourse on eschatological peace and on a hospitable welcome that nothing precedes, not even the origin, might be understood as anything but political irenism.

That war still bears witness to peace, that it remains a phenomenon of peace, is not, as we know, one of the consequences drawn by Levinas, but the risk remains. In any event, we are clearly told that allergy, the inhospitable forgetting of the transcendence of the Other, this forgetting of language, in short, is still a testimony, an unconscious testimony, if such a thing is possible: it *attests* to the very thing it forgets, namely, transcendence, separation, and thus language and hospitality, as well as woman and the father. That is what "remains [*demeure*]" "in its dwelling [*demeure*]."

> But the separated being can close itself up in its egoism, that is, in the very accomplishment of its isolation. And this possibility of forgetting the transcendence of the Other—of banishing with impunity all hospitality (that is, all language) from one's home, banishing the transcendental relation that alone permits the I to shut itself up in itself—*attests* to the absolute truth, the radicalism, of separation. Separation is not only dialectically correlative with transcendence, as its reverse; it is accomplished as a positive event. The relation with infinity remains [*demeure*] as another possibility of the being recollected in its dwelling [*sa demeure*]. The possibility for the home to open to the Other is as essential to the essence of the home as closed doors and windows.[103]

If language or the transcendence of the Other *are* or *translate* hospitable friendship itself, then the interpretation of this translation distinguishes in a troubling fashion (troubling because, as we began to see a moment ago, this distinction constantly risks being effaced) the Levinasian concept of "peace" from the Kantian one. This paradoxical legacy of Kant seems to be evoked in a sort of wry allusion to the peace of cemeteries that *Toward Perpetual Peace* also treats with irony. For Levinas, as for Kant, eternal peace must remain a peace of the living.

To define a pluralism of radical separation, a pluralism in which the plurality is not that of a total community, that of the cohesion or coherence of the whole, "the coherence of the elements that constitute plurality," it is necessary to think plurality as peace:

> The unity of plurality is peace, and not the coherence of the elements that constitute plurality. Peace therefore cannot be

identified with the end of combats that cease for want of combatants, by the defeat of some and the victory of the others, that is, with cemeteries or future universal empires. Peace must be my peace, in a relation that starts from an I and goes to the other, in desire and goodness, where the I both maintains itself and exists without egoism.[104]

The Preface of *Totality and Infinity* already denounces the "peace of empires"—about which there would still be much to say today, well beyond the *pax romana*: "The peace of empires issued from war rests on war."

This concept of peace seems to move at once toward and away from Kant, who is himself at once Christian and a man of the Enlightenment, who thinks peace in a purely political fashion and always on the basis of the State, even if the notion of the political in this politics is always inadequate to itself. The insistent critique of the State in *Totality and Infinity* regularly calls into question the "tyranny of the State" as well as the "anonymous universality of the State."[105] The becoming political of hospitality, its becoming part of the State, is no doubt a response to an aspiration; it corresponds, moreover, to the call of the third; but it "deforms the I and the other" and tends to introduce tyrannical violence. That is why politics must never be left "to itself." It would always judge "in absentia," always judge only the dead or the absent, where the face is not present, where there is no one to say "Here I am." This might be the place for a future meditation on what being "in absentia" might mean in relation to law and to politics, beyond the striking though fleeting use Levinas makes of this word or figure.

Metaphysics, or the relation to the other, is accomplished as service and as *hospitality*. Insofar as the face of the Other relates us to the *third*, the metaphysical relation of the I to the

Other moves into the form of the We, *aspires* to a State, institutions, laws, which are the source of universality. But *politics left to itself bears a tyranny within itself*; it *deforms* the I and the other who have given rise to it, for it judges them according to universal rules, and thus as *in absentia* [par contumace].[106]

The political dissimulates because it brings to light. It hides what it throws light on. Giving the face to be seen, bringing or attracting it into the space of public phenomenality, it thereby renders it invisible. Visibility renders invisible its invisibility, that is, the withdrawal of its epiphany. But exhibiting the invisibility of the face is not the only way of dissimulating it. The violence of the political mistreats the face yet again by effacing its unicity in a generality. These two violences are in the end the same, and Levinas associates them when he speaks of "attention to the Other as unicity and face (which the visibleness of the political leaves invisible), which can be produced only in the unicity of an I." He then immediately adds, pointing in the direction of a certain interpretation of Kierkegaard or Rosenzweig, the clarification that we must cite and situate one more time, so as now to emphasize a certain "perhaps": "Subjectivity is thus rehabilitated in the work of truth, and not as an egoism refusing the system which offends it. Against this egoist protestation of the subjectivity, against this protestation in the first person, the universalism of Hegelian reality will *perhaps* prevail."[107]

"Perhaps"; but then perhaps it is also more difficult for the State to be denounced, or indeed delimited.

Clearly, there can be no peace worthy of its name in the space of this "tyranny" or this "anonymous universality." But as we have come to suspect, the topology of this politics is rather convoluted. Levinas acknowledges that what "identifies itself outside of the State" (peace, hospitality, paternity, infinite fecundity, etc.) has a framework *in* the State, "identifies itself outside of the State, even if the State reserves a framework for it."

There is thus a topological destiny for this structural complication of the political. We spoke earlier of an enclave of transcendence. The border between the ethical and the political here loses for good the indivisible simplicity of a limit. No matter what Levinas might have said, the determinability of this limit was never pure, and it never will be. It would be possible to follow this inclusion of excess, or this transcendence in immanence, through subsequent texts such as "Beyond the State in the State" or "The State of Caesar and the State of David." A hyperbolic transgression brings about a disjunction in the immanence to self. In each case, this disjunction has to do with the pre-originary ex-propriety or ex-appropriation that makes of the subject a guest [*hôte*] and an hostage, someone who is, *before* every invitation, elected, invited, *and* visited in his home as in the home of the other, who is *in his own home in the home of the other*, in a given *at home*, an at home that is given or, rather, loaned, allotted, advanced before every contract, in the "anachronism of a debt preceding the loan."[108]

According to the logic of this advance, a logic that is at once peaceful, gentle, and ineluctable, the welcoming one is welcomed. He is first welcomed by the face of the other whom he means to welcome. Although this peace is neither political, nor related to the state, nor, in the language of Kant, cosmopolitical, that does not prevent Levinas from using language that resonates with Kant's. This occurs in the ironic allusion to the cemetery, to a peace that must not be the peace of the dead. As is often the case, Levinas is eager to remain on Kant's side. He speaks in Kant's direction, even if he is not strictly speaking or totally Kantian—indeed far from it—and he does so at the very moment he is opposing Kant.

In this sarcastic staging by Kant, I will emphasize something that disappears like a detail to which one pays hardly any attention. The allusion to the peace of cemeteries refers to an innkeeper, a hosteler, the sign of an inn that takes in and gives shelter. We are welcomed at the very outset under the sign of a sign of hospitality, at the sign of hospitality, by the witty remark of a hosteler, the questionable words of a host or the bad humor of an innkeeper (*Gastwirt*). Already in the Foreword, on the threshold, therefore, of *Toward Perpetual Peace*, we find ourselves received by a prefatory warning. Before this, there is the title, which does more than one thing: it situates and announces a place, the perpetual peace that will be treated—which is also the refuge or the inn. In the process, it promises, greets, dedicates: *Zum Ewigen Frieden* (To perpetual peace or for perpetual peace). Kant's first words thus put us on guard against the confusion between two peaces, the refuge and the cemetery:

> One may leave in suspense [*Ob . . . mag dahin gestellt werden*: the question of knowing whether . . . can be left in suspense, like a title or a sign] the question of whether this satirical inscription on a Dutch innkeeper's sign [*auf dem Schilde jenes holländischen Gastwirts*] upon which a burial ground was painted had for its object *mankind* in general, or the rulers of states in particular, who are insatiable of war, or merely *the* philosophers [*die Philosophen*] who dream this sweet dream.

Zum ewigen Frieden would thus be the ambiguous promise of a perpetual or eternal peace, the equivocal or hypocritical promise of a hospitality without restriction. But Kant wants neither the cemetery with which the rulers of States and the hawks of every epoch threaten us nor the "sweet dream" of the pacifist philosopher, an idealistic and impotent utopia, an oneiric irenism. The law and cosmopolitics of hospitality that he proposes in response to this terrible alternative is a set of rules and contracts, an interstate conditionality that limits, against the backdrop of natural law reinterpreted within a Christian horizon, the very hospitality it guarantees. The right to refuge is very strictly delimited by such rules. There is not enough time, and this is not the place, to analyze this text more closely. Our task here is simply—between Kant and Levinas—to sharpen a difference that matters today more than ever with regard to this right of refuge and all the most urgent matters of our time, everywhere that—in Israel, in Rwanda, in Europe, in America, in Asia, and in all the Churches of St. Bernard in the world—millions of "undocumented immigrants" [*sans papiers*], of "homeless" [*sans domicile fixe*], call out for another international law, another border politics, another humanitarian politics, indeed a humanitarian commitment that *effectively* operates beyond the interests of Nation-States.

VI

Let us return for a moment to Jerusalem.

"We are approaching the gates of Jerusalem."

What is an approach? Will such an approach ever end?

Let us go to Jerusalem, one year after this separation of separation, one year after the death of Emmanuel Levinas.

The *A-dieu* of separation leaves us still this grace, this to be thankful for, thanks to him, to be able to understand, read, welcome and receive him according to the trace.

We might meditate upon—and thus affirm—the possibility of such a chance.

Once sealed in this writing, once and for all, the *Saying à-Dieu* crosses in one word, but *to infinity*, greeting and the promise, welcome [*bienvenue*] and separation: the welcome at the heart of separation, of holy separation. At the moment of death, but also in the encounter with the other at this very moment, in the gesture of welcoming—and always to infinity: *Adieu.*

To infinity, surely, because the *à-Dieu* says first of all "the idea of infinity."

In this sense, it is also a kind of bidding *adieu* to Descartes. As was suggested earlier, Descartes would probably have hesitated to go along with Levinas in this sort of turning aside or redirecting of the tradition concerning the idea of infinity in me. It is important then to note the exact nature of this redirection, and to describe the movement by which Levinas separates himself from Descartes. It is in order to Say *à-Dieu*, to-God, the *to*, the *à*, of *à-Dieu*, the turn and the turning aside of this *to*, and to do so at the very moment of explaining what "did not interest Descartes, for whom the mathematical clarity and distinctness of ideas was enough," since the whole paradox of the idea of infinity was "subordinated in the Cartesian system to the search for knowledge." Acknowledging the analogy between his critique and the one leveled by Husserl against Descartes, though confirming the phenomenological interruption of phenomenology that we spoke of earlier, Levinas calls the *à-Dieu* an "extraordinary structure of the idea of infinity" that coincides neither with the "self-identification of identity" nor with "self-consciousness." That is because the *à*, the "to"—and this is its turn—itself turns toward infinity. Even before *itself* turning in this way, it is *turned*: by Infinity toward infinity. Even though it cannot, by definition, measure up to this measureless-ness or excess—for Levinas notes in passing the inadequa-tion of *à* in the French language, and he does so at the very moment when, in this very language, he invents this re-course for it.[109] The preposition *à* is preposed *à l'infini*, to the infinite that is preposed in it. The *à*, the *to*, is not only open to infinity, uniquely open, *that is to Say to God* [*c'est à Dire à Dieu*], *said otherwise*, it turns in its direction and addresses itself, *first so as to respond to it, first so as to be re-sponsible for it*, it addresses its *ad* to [*à*] the infinite that calls it and addresses itself to it; it opens the reference-*to* [*à*], the relation-*to* [*à*], *to* the infinity of its bearing. It has, from the beginning, before everything, before giving or giving pardon to God, before belonging to God, before anything whatsoever, before being itself, before any pre-sent, *destined* [*voué*] it to the excess of a desire—the desire called *A-Dieu*. God resides in this, God who *desires to re-side there*: the desire says *A-Dieu*.

> It is not in the finality of an intentional aim that I think in-finity. My most profound thought, the one that bears all thought, my thought of infinity older than the thought of the finite, is the very diachrony of time, non-coincidence, divest-ment itself: a way of "being destined" before any act of con-sciousness . . . A way of being destined or devoted that is de-votion itself. *A Dieu*, which is precisely not intentionality in its noetic-noematic form. . . . The *à-Dieu* or the idea of Infinity is not a species of some genre like intentionality or aspiration. The dynamism of *desire* refers on the contrary to the *à-Dieu*, a thought that is more profound and older than the cogito.[110]

Why name desire here? Why say in what it resides or *desires to reside*? And why associate it with the name of Jerusalem, with a certain desire *of* Jerusalem? With desir-ing as the desire to reside there?

We do so at the moment of concluding a discourse on

the ethics and politics of hospitality. Before attempting to respond to the above questions, I would recall this indication: Levinas often, at the moment of saying in what the *à-Dieu* resides, evokes in God the love of the stranger. God would be above all, it is said, the one "who loves the stranger."[111] Excessively so, for the excess is also, like the *non-reciprocity* that is decided in death (which is why the salutation is an *adieu*), like the interruption of symmetry or of commensurability, the trait or stroke, the uniting stroke, the hyphen [*trait d'union*] that separates the *adieu*, the hyphen of the *à-Dieu*. A-Dieu beyond being, where God not only does not have to exist but where he does not have to give to me or give me pardon. What would faith or devotion be when directed toward a God who would not be able to abandon me? Of whom I would be absolutely certain, assured of his concern? A God who could not but give to me or give of himself to me? Who could not not choose me? Would Levinas have endorsed these last propositions, namely, that the *à-Dieu*, like salutation or prayer, must be addressed to a God who not only might not exist (who might no longer or not yet exist) but who might abandon me and not turn toward me through any covenant or election?

Desire, love of the stranger, excess: that is what I wanted, under the title or in the name of the *Adieu*, to put as an exergue to this conclusion—approaching Jerusalem.

"God who loves the stranger," rather than shows himself—is this not, beyond being and the phenomenon, beyond being and nothingness, a God who, although he literally *is* not, not "contaminated by being," would destine the *à-Dieu*, the salutation and the holy separation to desire as "love of the stranger"? Before and beyond the "existence" of God, outside of his probable improbability, right up to the most vigilant if not the most desperate, the most "sober," of atheisms (Levinas likes this word "sober [*dé-grisé*]"), the Saying *à-Dieu* would signify hospitality. This is not some abstraction that one would call, as I have just hastily done, "love of the stranger," but (God) "*who* loves the stranger."

Who loves the stranger. Who loves the *stranger*? Whom else is there *to love*?

∽

Let us return for a moment to Jerusalem.

Let us go to Jerusalem.

To Jerusalem; perhaps we are there.

Is the step [*pas*] of such a return possible? The possibility is measured here against the effectivity of a promise. Certainly. A promise remains, its possibility remains effective, but ethics demands that this effectivity be effectuated, without which the promise betrays the promise by renouncing what it promises. Is the realization of an effective possibility of ethics already politics? Which politics?

We are there, in the earthly Jerusalem, between war and peace, in this war that is called from every side without anyone believing it, without anyone making us believe it, the "peace process." We are in a promise that is at once threatened and threatening, in the present without present, in the imminence of a promised Jerusalem.

"What is promised in Jerusalem is a humanity of the Torah," Emmanuel Levinas once said.

What does this mean? Who are the *hôtes* and the hostages of Jerusalem? How is one to understand the "humanity of the Torah" when, in order to determine the promise that bears this place name, Jerusalem, Levinas insists on the earth, on the "earthly Jerusalem" and not the heavenly one, a Jerusalem "not outside all places, in pious thoughts."[112]

Why gesture in the direction of a welcome that would be more than a welcome, older or more to come than a welcome? An eschatological hospitality that would be more than hospitality, as it is understood in law and in politics, a hospitality *of* the Torah that would be, in a word, more than a refuge? Why should the ethics of hospitality be something more and something other than a law or politics of refuge?

These questions are not posed.

Or at least they are never posed in the repose of a place. They put one to the test of an interrogation that endures them without repose.

So as to evoke this endurance (what else can be done here in just a few minutes?), let us simply mark a few stages in the extraordinary itinerary of reading and interpretation that we should follow word by word, step by step, in *Beyond the Verse*, especially in chapter 3, entitled "Cities of Refuge."[113]

It consists of about twenty pages. The subtle movement of this exegesis is at once varied, patient, inventive, cautious, *and* risky, as well as open, its breath held—suspended—to such a degree that I hesitate to take the risk of stopping it or even momentarily breaking it up according to the crude pedagogy of a series of stages or arguments. I will make the attempt nonetheless, but only so as to invite you, as an opening, to return to what is announced in this place.

Perhaps it will suffice to recall, by means of an ellipsis, the feminine figure of Jerusalem. It would reawaken what was heard earlier, and questioned, concerning hospitality and the feminine being who would be "hospitable welcome par excellence," "the welcoming one par excellence," "welcoming in itself."

To desire, to reside. In singing the election of Zion by

the desire of Yahweh—yes, the *desire* of Yahweh—a psalm (132: 13) names Jerusalem as the chosen lover or spouse for a dwelling. God says that he *desires to reside* in Zion. "There I will reside, for I desired it," says one translation. Desiring to reside, as if it were a single word, a single and same movement, for there is no desire without this elective claim, without this exclusive request for a singular residence.

> Yes, Yahweh has chosen Zion; he has desired it for his habitation.
> This is my resting place forever; here I will reside, for I have desired it.[114]

Does Levinas say anything else but this when, following the figure of another psalm (122: 3), he describes a Jerusalem "built as a city that is bound firmly together," bound between the heavenly height of God and the earthy realm below?

Running through two interpretations of this figure, the Zionist and the universalist, Levinas prefers a third meaning, according to which there is no religious salvation (the vertical dimension) without justice in the earthly city and the human dwelling (the horizontal dimension). It is toward this "third meaning" that a meditation begins to unfold on the Jerusalem of the Torah "in the context of this humanist urbanism of the cities of refuge,"[115] this "humanism or humanitarianism of the cities of refuge."[116]

An increasing number of allusions follow to what "topical significance [this] might have for us,"[117] to the "spirit of revolt or even of delinquency in our suburbs, the result of the social imbalance in which we are placed." "Does not all this make our cities," Levinas asks, "cities of refuge or cites of exiles?"[118]

This reading of an excerpt from Tractate Makkoth, 10a,

focuses more specifically on the notion of cities of refuge, which, according to Numbers 35, God commands Moses to open up to anyone who has killed unintentionally and is being pursued by an avenger of blood or "ransomer of blood" (as Chouraqui translates it). One is to offer shelter to the involuntary murderer being pursued by the "avenger of blood" so as to secure his safety. One is to stop at the city gates an avenger who feels justified in seeking his own justice when the tribunal remains powerless to judge someone who is guilty "inadvertently," someone who has killed without the intention of causing death.

Levinas's first concern is to note that this divine injunction commands the creation of a right—in truth, a counter-right—that sanctions the protection of the involuntary murderer against the "marginal right" of the avenger of blood. The jurisdiction of this counter-right, which is praised by Levinas, is rather refined, because by limiting the time of asylum offered to the murderer it allows asylum to be turned into exile—and hospitality into punishment. For the objective or involuntary murder does not have to be totally excused. Levinas insists on this double finality. Indeed, it is there to remind us that there is no real discontinuity between voluntary and involuntary murder. Sometimes invisible, always to be deciphered, this continuity forces us to infinitize our responsibility: we are also responsible for our lack of attention and for our carelessness, for what we do neither intentionally nor freely, indeed, for what we do unconsciously—since this is never without significance. Further on, there appears a more radical formulation: "there would be only one race of murderers, whether the murder is committed involuntarily or intentionally."[119]

But this is only the first stage. In the wake of another verse, Levinas asks why it is prescribed that a master of the

Torah follow his disciple when the disciple must go into exile in a city of refuge. Are we to conclude from this that the Torah itself needs to be protected and offered asylum through exile in a city of refuge? "Is the Torah not a city of refuge?," Levinas then asks.

> Is this not known by the following "questionable" herme- neutic [a bit later he will call it "specious"]:
>
> "But that cannot be correct, seeing that Rabbi Johanan said: Whence can it be shown (Scripturally) that the study of the Torah affords asylum? From the verse: 'Bezer in the wilderness' (Deuteronomy 4: 43) [that Moses chose], which is followed by: 'This is the law [Torah] which Moses set be- fore the children of Israel'(Deuteronomy 4: 44)."[120]

After having given some credit to this "specious" inter- pretation, after having glossed and discussed it, Levinas takes a further step. This step would carry us beyond "the noble lesson of the city of refuge, its indulgence and its forgiveness." In spite of the juridical refinement it intro- duces, indeed because of this very casuistry, the "noble les- son" remains equivocal with regard to the Torah. The Torah demands more; it demands more from Jerusalem, requires more in Jerusalem.

> The Torah is justice, a complete justice which goes beyond the ambiguous situations of the cities of refuge. A complete justice because, in its expressions and contents, it is a call for absolute vigilance. The great awakening from which all over- sight, even that of involuntary murder, is excluded. Jerusalem will be defined by this Torah, a city consequently of extreme consciousness. As if the consciousness of our habitual life were still asleep, as if we had not yet got a foothold in reality.
>
> We are approaching the gates [*portes*] of Jerusalem.[121]

A complete justice, Torah-of-Jerusalem, but a justice whose extreme vigilance requires that it become effective,

that it make itself into law and politics. Once again, beyond the State *in* the State, beyond law *in* the law, responsibility held hostage to the here-now, the law of justice that transcends the political and the juridical, in the
philosophical sense of these terms, must bend to itself, to
the point of exceeding and obsessing it, everything that
the face exceeds, in the face to face or in the interruption
of the third that marks the demand for justice as law.

It is right endlessly to insist on this: even if the experience of the third, the origin of justice and of the question
as a putting into question, is defined as the interruption of
the face to face, it is not an intrusion that comes second.
The experience of the third is *ineluctable* from the very
first moment, and ineluctable in the face; even if it interrupts the face to face, it also belong to it; as self-interrup-
tion it belongs to the face and can be produced only
through it: "The revelation of the third, ineluctable in the
face, is produced only through the face."[122]

It is as if the unicity of the face were, in its absolute and
irrecusable singularity, plural *a priori*. As we have insisted,
Levinas already takes this into account, so to speak, in *Totality and Infinity*,[123] well before the "logic" of substitution, already sketched out in 1961,[124] gets developed in
Otherwise than Being. The most general possibility of substitution, a simultaneous condition, a paradoxical reciprocity (the condition of irreciprocity) of the unique and
of its replacement, a place that is at once untenable and
assigned, the placement of the singular as replaceable, the
irrecusable place of the neighbor and of the third—is not
all this the first affection of the subject in its ipseity? Thus
understood, substitution announces the destiny of subjectivity, the subjection of the subject, as host or hostage:
"The subject is a host" (*Totality and Infinity*); "the subject
is hostage" (*Otherwise than Being*). As host or hostage, as

other, as pure alterity, a subjectivity analyzed in this way must be stripped of every ontological predicate, a bit like the pure I that Pascal said is stripped of every quality that could be attributed to it, of every property that, as pure I, as properly pure, it would have to transcend or exceed. And the other is not reducible to its actual predicates, to what one might define or thematize about it, anymore than the I is. It is naked, bared of every property, and this nudity is also its infinitely exposed vulnerability: its skin. This absence of determinable properties, of concrete predicates, of empirical visibility, is no doubt what gives to the face of the other a spectral aura, especially if the subjectivity of the *hôte* also lets itself be announced as the visitation of a face, of a visage. *Host* or *guest* [in English], *Gastgeber* or *Gast*, the *hôte* would be not only a hostage. It would have, according to a profound necessity, at least the face or figure of a spirit or phantom (*Geist, ghost*). When someone once expressed concern to Levinas about the "phantomatic character" of his philosophy, especially when it treats the "face of the other," Levinas did not directly object. Resorting to what I have just called the "Pascalian" argument ("it is necessary that the other be welcomed independently of his qualities"), he clearly specified "welcomed," especially in an "immediate," urgent way, without waiting, as if "real" qualities, attributes, or properties (everything that makes a living person into something other than a phantom) slowed down, mediatized, or compromised the purity of this welcome. It is necessary to welcome the other in his alterity, without waiting, and thus not to pause to recognize his real predicates. It is thus necessary, beyond all perception, to receive the other while running the risk, a risk that is always troubling, strangely troubling, like the stranger (*unheimlich*), of a hospitality offered to the *guest* as *ghost* or *Geist* or *Gast*. There would be no hospitality without the chance of spectrality. But spectrality is not nothing, it exceeds, and thus deconstructs, all ontological oppositions, being and nothingness, life and death—and it also gives. It can give [*donner*], give order(s) [*ordonner*] and give pardon [*pardonner*], and it can also not do so, like God beyond essence. God without being, God uncontaminated by being—is this not the most rigorous definition of the Face of the Wholly Other? But is this not then an apprehension that is as spectral as it is spiritual?

Is it insignificant that the city of refuge is first of all more than a promise? It is an order given in a situation where death was dealt or given without the intention of giving it. But it is also the order to save from death a murderer haunted by the spectral return of the victim, by the revenge of the phantom, by avengers bent on dealing death in their turn. Whence its extreme ambiguity: shelter must be given to one who is guilty of an involuntary act, immunity, at least a temporary immunity, must be granted to a murderer.

Though it exceeds the political ambiguity or juridical equivocation to which the "noble lesson" of the cities of refuge still bears witness, the Torah, the Torah in Jerusalem, the Torah-Jerusalem, must still inscribe the promise *in* the earthly Jerusalem. And henceforth command the comparison of incomparables (the definition of justice, of the concession made, out of duty, to synchrony, co-presence, the system, and, finally, the State). It must enjoin a negotiation with the non-negotiable so as to find the "better" or the least bad.

Nothing counts more, nothing weighs more heavily, than the quotation marks around the word "better" [*meilleur*] here, the best [*meilleur*] word. Political civilization, says Levinas, is "better" than barbarism, but it is only "better," that is, less bad. It is not good, it is only a stopgap, but one that *it is necessary* to seek, that it is necessary not to stop seeking. For the conclusion of this text once again cautions us against a Zionism that would be simply a politics, just "one more nationalism or particularism":

> It is precisely in contrast to the cities of refuge that this claim of the Torah through which Jerusalem is defined can be understood. The city of refuge is the city of a civilization or of a humanity which protects subjective innocence and forgives objective guilt and all the denials that acts inflict on intentions. A political civilization, 'better' than that of passions and so-called free desires, which, abandoned to the hazards of their eruptions, end up in a world where, according to an expression from the Pirqe Aboth, "men are ready to swallow each other alive." A civilization of the law, admittedly, but a political civilization whose justice is hypocritical and where, with an undeniable right, the avenger of blood prowls.
>
> What is promised in Jerusalem, on the other hand, is a humanity of the Torah. It will have been able to surmount the deep contradictions of the cities of refuge: a new humanity that is better than a Temple. Our text, which began with the cities of refuge, reminds us or teaches us that the *longing* for Zion, that Zionism, is not one more nationalism or particularism; nor is it a simple search for a place of refuge. It is the *hope* of a science of society, and of a society, which are wholly human. And this hope is to be found in Jerusalem, in the earthly Jerusalem, and not outside all places, in pious thoughts.[125]

Can we not hear this promise?

We can also receive and listen to it. We can even feel ourselves engaged by it without, however, remaining insensitive to the silence it bears at the heart of the call. This silence can also be the figure of a hiatus, that is, a mouth opened to speak and to eat, but a mouth that is still silent.

As for me, I believe I hear such a silence in this conclusion that speaks of a "hope" beyond "refuge." For nothing is determined here, I would even say determinable, concerning the "better" politics, the "better" law, be this the law of war or the law of nations [*le droit des gens*], that, in a world where the law of modern Nation-States reigns, in a "hypocritical" "political civilization," and in the earthly Jerusalem of today and tomorrow, would respond "best" or least poorly to this promise.

To put this in the terms of a classical philosophical discourse, silence is kept concerning the rules or schemas (there would be none for pure practical reason, according to Kant) that would procure for us "better" or less bad mediations: between ethics or the holiness of messianic hospitality on the one hand and the "peace process," the process of political peace, on the other.

∼

This silence comes to us from the abyss.

It perhaps resembles, it perhaps echoes—just perhaps—the silence from the depths of which Elijah heard himself called, him alone ("How is it, Elijah, that you're here; what are you *doing* here?"), from the depths of a voice that was scarcely a voice, an almost inaudible voice, a voice barely to be distinguished from a light breeze, a voice as subtle as silence, "a sound of sheer silence," but a voice that Elijah thought he could make out after having sought in vain the presence of God on the mountain, in the wind, then in the earthquake, and then in the fire, a voice that asks ("What are you doing here?") and that orders, "Go."[126]

More intractable than the wind, the earthquake, and the fire, the silence of this voice is not just any abyss, and it is not necessarily a bad abyss. One might even try to discern its edges. It does not whisper silence over the necessity of a *relation* between ethics and politics, ethics and justice or law. *This relation is necessary*, it must exist, it is necessary to deduce a politics and a law from ethics. This deduction is necessary in order to determine the "better" or the "less bad," with all the requisite quotation marks: democracy is "better" than tyranny. Even in its "hypocritical" nature, "political civilization" remains "better" than barbarism.

What consequences should be drawn from this? Would Levinas have subscribed to those we risked formulating earlier, or those we are advancing now? Whatever our desire for fidelity, we cannot respond to this question, we *must* not claim to do so, or claim responsibility for what Levinas himself would have responded. Concerning, for example, what was said earlier about the perjury of justice and everything that then follows, where I interpret this silence between ethics and politics, ethics and law.

How is one to hear this silence? Who can hear it?

It seems to dictate this to me: the *formal* injunction of the deduction remains irrecusable, and it does not wait any more than the third and justice do. Ethics enjoins a politics and a law: this dependence and the direction of this conditional derivation are as irreversible as they are unconditional. But the political or juridical *content* that is thus assigned remains undetermined, still to be determined beyond knowledge, beyond all presentation, all concepts, all possible intuition, in a singular way, in the speech and the responsibility *taken* by each person, in each situation, and on the basis of an analysis that is each time unique—unique and infinite, unique but *a priori* exposed to substitution,[127] unique and yet general, interminable in spite of the urgency of the decision. For the

analysis of a context and of political motivations can have
no end as soon as it includes in its calculations a limitless
past and future. As always, the decision remains heterogeneous to the calculations, knowledge, science, and consciousness that nonetheless condition it. The silence of
which we are speaking, the one toward which we are above
all attentive, is the elementary and decisive between-time,
the meantime, the instantaneous meantime of decision,
which unsettles time and puts it off its hinges ("out of
joint") in anachrony and in contretemps: that is, when the
law of the law exposes itself, *of itself*, in the non-law, by becoming at once host and hostage, the host and hostage of
the other, when the law of the unique must give itself over
to substitution and to the law of generality—without
which one would obey an ethics without law—when the
"Thou shall not kill," wherein both the Torah and the law
of messianic peace are gathered, still allows any State (the
one of Caesar or the one of David, for example) to feel
justified in raising an army, in making war or keeping law
and order, in controlling its borders—in killing. Let's not
insist too much here on the obvious, but let's not forget it
too quickly, either.

~

The silence out of which we speak is surely not foreign
to the non-response by which Levinas often defines the
dead, or death, a death that does not signify nothingness.
This non-response, this interruption of the response, does
not await death without speech; it spaces and makes discontinuous all speech. The hiatus, the silence of this non-
response concerning the schemas between the ethical and
the political, remains. It is a fact that it remains, and this
fact is not some empirical contingency; it is a *Faktum*.

But it must also remain between the messianic promise

and the determination of a rule, norm, or political law. It marks a heterogeneity, a discontinuity between two orders, even if this be on the inside of the earthly Jerusalem. It marks the between-time or meantime of an indecision, the only basis on which responsibility and the decision are to be *taken* and determined. It is on the basis of this non-response that speech or words [*la parole*] may be *taken*, and first of all *given*, that anyone might claim to "take up speech," or take the floor in politics, out of fidelity to a speech or word that is given, to this giving of one's word, to the "word of honor" that we mentioned in the beginning.

This silence is thus also that of a speech or word that is given.

It gives speech, gives over speech; it is the gift of speech.

This non-response conditions my responsibility, there where I alone must respond. Without silence, without the hiatus, which is not the absence of rules but the necessity of a leap at the moment of ethical, political, or juridical decision, we could simply unfold knowledge into a program or course of action. Nothing could make us more irresponsible; nothing could be more totalitarian.

This discontinuity, moreover, allows us to subscribe to everything Levinas says about peace or messianic hospitality, about the beyond of the political in the political, without necessarily sharing all the "opinions" in his discourse having to do with an intrapolitical analysis of real situations or of what is actually going on today with the earthly Jerusalem, or indeed with a Zionism that would no longer be just one more nationalism (for we now know better than ever that all nationalisms like to think of themselves as universal in an exemplary fashion, that each claims this exemplarity and likes to think of itself as more than just one more nationalism). Even if, *in fact*, it seems difficult to maintain a faith in election, and especially in the election of an eternal people, safe from all "nationalist" (in the modern sense of this word) temptation, even if it seems difficult to dissociate them in the actual political situation of any Nation-State (and not just Israel), it is necessary to acknowledge that Levinas always wanted to protect the thematic of election (which is so central, so strong, and so determining in his work) from every nationalist seduction. One could cite any number of texts to prove this. Let it suffice to recall, among the extraordinary political essays written by Levinas between 1935 and 1939,[128] those that always placed the Covenant above or beyond a "Jewish nationalism."[129]

The same hiatus frees space; it can give its place to a subtle, difficult, but necessary analytical dissociation in the structure of arguments and the placement of statements. For example, in the discourse of Levinas. Dare I say that I never forgo, and, I believe, in the admiring fidelity and respect that I owe Emmanuel Levinas, must never forgo, the right to this analysis, indeed, to the discussion of some proposition or other in a text that cannot be homogeneous because it knows how to interrupt itself? For this same text gives to be thought, let us not forget, the contradiction internal to Saying, what we earlier called ContraDiction, an intimate caesura but also the inspiration and elementary respiration of Saying.

Isn't this discussion necessary precisely there where it is a question of responsibility before the other, in the face to face or in the attention to the third, in the very place where justice is non-dialectizable contra-diction?

The same duty to analyze would lead me to dissociate, with all the consequences that might follow, a structural messianicity, an irrecusable and threatening promise, an eschatology without teleology, from every determinate messianism: a messianicity before or without any messianism incorporated by some revelation in a determined place that goes by the name of Sinai or Mount Horeb.

But is it not Levinas himself who will have made us dream, in more than one sense of this word, of a revelation of the Torah before Sinai? Or, more precisely, of a *recognition* [*reconnaissance*] of the Torah before this revelation?

As for Sinai, the proper name *Sinai*, does it carry a metonymy? Or an allegory?[130] The nominal body of a barely decipherable interpretation that would come to recall to us, without forcing our certitude, what will have come *before* Sinai, at once the face, the withdrawal of the face, and what, in the name of the Third, that is to say, in the name of justice, contradicts the Saying in the Saying? Sinai: ContraDiction itself.

What I would have wanted to suggest, in short, has come to tremble here, and perhaps to communicate in trembling, a concern, a fear and trembling before what "Sinai," the proper name "Sinai," means, before what is called and calls us in this way, before what responds to this name, is responsible for this name, beginning from this name.

The proper name "Sinai" is thus just as enigmatic as the name "face." In the singular and the plural, retaining the memory of its Hebraic synonym, what is here called "face" also starts to resemble some untranslatable proper name. But this would be so only by virtue of an event of translation.

Of an *other translation*, an other thought of translation. Without anything just before, beginning from what is before the just before. Without original, beginning from what is pre-originary. For is not *visage* ["face"], or *visages* ["faces"]—which should be written at once in the singular and the plural, according to the unique, according to the face to face and according to the more-than-two of the third—also more than a very old name, a singular plural reinvented in the French language, a poem giving accord in turn to another French language, giving it to us by composing in it a new accord, a language that is still unheard of for the other man, for man as other or stranger, for the other to man, the other *of* man or the other *than* man?

Yes, such nomination would have been accorded to the French language. It was translated there, having visited this language, and now it is its hostage, like a proper name that is untranslatable outside the French language.

In this story, who was the host and who the guest? Who will be?

The word *à-Dieu* belongs to the same accord. Before the name or noun, before the verb, from the depths of the call or of the silent salutation, it comes to nomination to call the name by name. Without a name or noun, without a verb, so close to silence. *A-Dieu* is accorded to the face.

And "we meet death in the face of the Other."[131]

We recalled earlier the infinite meaning of the *à-Dieu*, the idea of infinity that exceeds the thought of it, as well as the *cogito*, noetic-noematic intentionality, knowledge, objectivity, finality, etc. But the idiom would be neutralized were one simply to translate *à-Dieu* by "the idea of infinity in the finite," thus reducing its meaning to this idea, to this excess of meaning. One could then use this as a pretext for forgetting death. And yet all of Levinas's thought, from the beginning to the end, was a meditation on death, a meditation that diverted, disconcerted, and set beside itself everything in philosophy, from Plato to Hegel to Heidegger, that was also, and first of all, concerned with death, *epimeleia thanatou, Sein zum Tode*.

When Levinas reinvents the thought of the *à-Dieu*, he of course thinks everything we just recalled under this name, but he does so without distancing himself from what he had to teach about death, against or apart from the philosophical tradition. This is particularly evident in his courses on *Death and Time*, and especially in an article of 1983, "Non-Intentional Consciousness." The *à-Dieu* there does indeed bear witness to the surplus of an infinity of meaning, to the (no) more-meaning to infinity, but it does so, if I may put it this way, at the hour of death. At the hour of a death that it is no longer necessary to approach by means of the alternative between being and nothingness. At the hour of this death, the salutation and the call say *à-Dieu*. Levinas had just recalled the "extreme uprightness of the face," but also the "uprightness of an exposure to death, without defense" and "a request to me addressed from the depths of an absolute solitude." Through this request would come to me, but as an assignation, "what is called the word of God." It is given to be heard in the *à-Dieu*.

> The call of God does not establish between me and the One who has spoken to me a *relation*; it does not establish something that, on any account, would be a conjunction—a co-existence, a synchrony, even if ideal—between terms. Infinity would have no meaning for a thought that goes to the limit, and the *à-Dieu* is not a finality. It is perhaps this irreducibility of the *à-Dieu* or of the fear of God to eschatology, this irreducibility that interrupts within the human the consciousness that was on its way toward being in its ontological perseverance or toward death which it takes as the ultimate thought, that is signified, beyond being, by the word "glory." The alternative between being and nothingness is not ultimate. The *à-Dieu* is not a process of Being: in the call, I am referred back to the other human being through whom this call signifies, to the neighbor for whom I must fear.[132]

On the same score, Levinas sometimes made use of the word *à-Dieu* otherwise, in another register. He wanted to say the same thing, no doubt, but from a less magisterial height. In a sort of smiling murmur, he began at the same time, in the course of the same decade, to say *adieu* to life. Like someone who feels and knows that he is aging, and that time is *adieu*, he said what *à-Dieu* comes to mean at a certain age, and how he was using this word *à-Dieu*, everything that he put into it ("as I express myself now"), and which we have just recalled—for example, vulnerability: "I do not contest that we are in fact always in this world, but it is a world wherein we are altered. Vulnerability is being able to say *adieu* to this world. One says *adieu* to it in aging. Time endures by way of this *adieu* and by way of the *à-Dieu*."[133]

Once again the *à-Dieu* as time or, more precisely, as the future "according to the way that is proper to me and that consists in treating time on the basis of the other": "It [time] is, according to its meaning (if one can speak of a meaning without intentionality: without vision or even aim), patient awaiting of God, patience of excess (an *à-Dieu*, as I express myself now); but an awaiting where nothing is awaited."[134]

Let us leave the last word to Emmanuel Levinas. A word for the orphan, a word whose destination we would not want to divert by addressing it to this other orphan, the one who has been so from the very beginning, the one who has been orphaned from even the condition of being an orphan, this orphan without a father, if one can still say this, without a dead father, this orphan—he or she—for whom "infinite fecundity," "the infinity of paternity," and the "marvel of the family"[135] would remain a forbidden certainty, the place of an older and even more immemorial question, the urgency of a concern for a still insatiable hospitality.

We will thus keep, for the moment, to what Levinas says elsewhere, literally, on the subject of the "Sinai Revelation" of the Torah, and on the subject of a translation or a thought of translation *to be invented,* a bit like politics itself.

What is the meaning of that notion of the heavenly origin of the Torah? In the literal sense, of course, it is a reference to the Sinai Revelation, to the divine origin of the text. There is no question here of putting that meaning aside. But if it is not possible to describe the lived meaning of such terms, one can inquire about the experience in which it is approached. . . . *to seek a translation that the properly religious surplus of truth already presupposes.* . . . The Torah is transcendent and from heaven by its demands that clash, in the final analysis, with the pure ontology of the world. The Torah demands, in opposition to the natural perseverance of each being in his or her own being (a fundamental ontological law), *concern for the stranger, the widow and the orphan, a preoccupation with the other person.*[136]

Notes

Notes

Adieu

The following notes were created by Vanghélis Bitsoris for his Greek translation of *Adieu* (Athens: AGRA, 1996), then included in the French edition. [Existing English translations of texts by Levinas and others have been used whenever possible, though many have been slightly modified to suit the context of Derrida's argument.—Trans.]

1. Cf. Jacques Derrida, *The Gift of Death*, trans. David Wills (Chicago: University of Chicago Press, 1995), 47:

> It seems to me that *adieu* can mean at least three things:
>
> 1. The salutation or benediction given (before all constative language "adieu" can just as well signify "hello," "I can see you," "I see that you are there," I speak to you before telling you anything else—and in certain circumstances in French it happens that one says *adieu* at the moment of meeting rather than separation);
> 2. The salutation or benediction given at the moment of separation, of departure, sometimes forever (this can never in fact be excluded), without any return on this earth, at the moment of death;
> 3. The *a-dieu*, for God or before God and before anything else or any relation to the other, in every other adieu. Every relation to the other would be, before and after anything else, an adieu.

[In his translation of "Bad Conscience and the Inexorable" (see n. 11 below), Richard Cohen captures much of the semantic richness of *adieu* with the English idiom "God bless." For an excellent discussion of the *adieu*, see Hent de Vries, "Adieu, à dieu, a-Dieu," in *Ethics as First Philosophy*, ed. Adriaan Peperzak (New York: Routledge, 1995): 211–19. This discussion is expanded in de Vries's *Philosophy and the Turn to Religion* (Baltimore: The Johns Hopkins University Press, 1999) and his *Horror Religiosus* (Baltimore: The Johns Hopkins University Press, forthcoming); the latter contains an illuminating chapter on the present book in the context of Derrida's other recent writings on hospitality.—Trans.]

2. Emmanuel Levinas, "Four Talmudic Readings," in *Nine Talmudic Readings*, trans. Annette Aronowicz (Bloomington: Indiana University Press, 1990), 48.

3. This is in the second of the "Four Talmudic Readings."

4. Ibid., 48.

5. Ibid.

6. See, e.g., ibid., 50: "Certainly, my responsibility for everyone can also manifest itself by limiting itself: the ego may be called in the name of this unlimited responsibility to concern itself about itself as well."

7. "Have we been rash in affirming that the first word, the one which makes all the others possible, including the *no* of negativity and the 'in-between-the-two' which is 'the temptation of temptation,' is an unconditional *yes*?" (ibid., 49).

8. Ibid.

9. Ibid.

10. See ibid., 50.

11. Emmanuel Levinas, "Bad Conscience and the Inexorable," in *Face to Face with Levinas*, ed. Richard A. Cohen (Albany: SUNY Press, 1986), 38. This essay is included as the final section of "La conscience non-intentionnelle," in *Entre nous: Essais sur le penser-à-l'autre* (Paris: Grasset, 1991).

12. See, e.g., Emmanuel Levinas, *Totality and Infinity*, trans. Alphonso Lingis (Pittsburgh: Duquesne University Press, 1969), 177–79. In "The Trace of the Other" (orig. pub. 1963),

Levinas defines the work: "*A work conceived radically is a move-ment of the same unto the other which never returns to the same.* To the myth of Ulysses returning to Ithaca, we wish to oppose the story of Abraham, who leaves his fatherland forever for a yet unknown land, and forbids his servant to bring back even his son to the point of departure. A work conceived in its ulti-mate nature requires a radical generosity of the same, which in the work goes unto the other. It then requires an *ingratitude* of the other. Gratitude would in fact be the *return* of the move-ment to its origin." ("The Trace of the Other," trans. Alphonso Lingis, in *Deconstruction in Context*, ed. Mark C. Taylor [Chi-cago: University of Chicago Press, 1986], 348–49.) See also Jacques Derrida, "At This Very Moment in This Work Here I Am," trans. Ruben Berezdivin, in *Re-Reading Levinas*, ed. Rob-ert Bernasconi and Simon Critchley (Bloomington: Indiana University Press, 1991), 11–48.

13. See, e.g., *Totality and Infinity*, 267–69, where Levinas re-lates fecundity to the work.

14. Exodus 26: 31, 33. "You shall make a curtain of blue, pur-ple, and crimson yarns, and of fine twisted linen . . . and the curtain shall separate for you the holy place from the most holy." The opening of the tent was protected by a "screen" (*epis-pastron*, according to the Greek translation of the Septuagint), while inside the tent the "curtain" (*katapētasma*) of a veil sepa-rated "the holy and the holy of holies" (*to hagion kai to hagion tōn hagiōn*).

15. See Levinas's preface to Marlène Zarader, *Heidegger et les paroles de l'origine* (Paris: Vrin, 1986), 12–13. [See also the inter-view with Schlomo Malka published in *Les Nouveaux Cahiers* 18 (1982–3): 71, 1–8; trans. Jonathan Romney in *The Levinas Reader*, ed. Seán Hand (Cambridge, Mass.: Blackwell, 1989), 297.—Trans.]

16. See *Totality and Infinity*, 304–6.

17. This is one of two courses Levinas taught at the Sor-bonne (Paris IV) during 1975–76. It was first published in 1991 under the title "La mort et le temps" in *Emmanuel Levinas* (*Cahiers de l'Herne*, no. 60, 21–75), and then in 1993 (with the

other course from the same year: "Dieu et l'onto-théo-logie") in Levinas, *Dieu, la mort et le temps* (Paris: Grasset, 1993).

18. "In the duration of time, whose signification should perhaps not be referred to the pair being-nothingness as the ultimate reference of meaning, of all that is meaningful and all that is thought, of all that is human, death is a point from which time gets all its patience, this awaiting refusing itself to the intentionality of awaiting—'patience and length of time,' says the proverb, patience as the emphasis of passivity. Whence the direction of this course; death as the patience of time." (*Dieu, la mort et le temps*, 16.)

19. See ibid., 122: "We meet death in the face of the Other."

20. See ibid., 17: "Death is, in beings, the disappearance of the expressive movements that made them appear as living—movements that are always *responses*. Death will touch above all this autonomy or expressivity of movements that goes so far as to cover someone's face. Death is the *without-response*."

21. See ibid., 20: "Death is this irremediable gap: biological movements lose all their dependence upon signification or expression. Death is decomposition: it is the without-response."

22. Ibid., 47.

23. "Death is interpreted in the whole philosophical and religious tradition either as a passage to nothingness or as a passage to another existence, continuing in a new setting." (*Totality and Infinity*, 232.)

24. See ibid., 232: "More profoundly and as it were a priori we approach death as nothingness in the passion for murder. The spontaneous intentionality of this passion aims at annihilation. Cain, when he slew Abel, must have possessed such a knowledge of death. The identifying of death with nothingness befits the death of the other in murder."

25. See ibid., 232–33: "The identifying of death with nothingness befits the death of the other in murder. But at the same time this nothingness presents itself there as a sort of impossibility. For the Other cannot present himself as Other outside of my conscience, and his face expresses my moral impossibility of annihilating. This interdiction is to be sure not equivalent to

pure and simple impossibility, and even presupposes the possibility which precisely it forbids—but in fact the interdiction already dwells in this very possibility rather than presupposing it; it is not added to it after the event, but looks at me from the very depths of the eyes I want to extinguish, looks at me as the eye that in the tomb shall look at Cain."

26. See *Dieu, la mort et le temps*, 123: "To bring to the fore the question that death raises in the proximity of the neighbor, a question that, paradoxically, is my responsibility for his death. Death opens to the face of the Other, which is the expression of the commandment, 'Thou shall not kill.'"

27. See ibid., 23: "Death is at once healing and impotence; an ambiguity that perhaps indicates another dimension of meaning than the one whereby death is thought according to the alternative being/not-being. Ambiguity: enigma."

28. "Bad Conscience and the Inexorable," 40.

29. Levinas defines death as "ex-ception": "The relation with the death of the Other is neither a *knowledge* of the death of the Other nor the experience of this death in its very way of annihilating being (if, as is commonly thought, the event of this death can be reduced to such an annihilation). There is no knowledge of this ex-ceptional relation (ex-ception: to seize and put outside of the series)." (*Dieu, la mort et le temps*, 25.)

30. See ibid., 54: "It is the death of the other for which I am responsible, to the point of including myself in this death. This is perhaps shown in the more acceptable proposition: 'I am responsible for the other insofar as he is mortal.' The death of the other is the first death."

31. See ibid., 31 and 199: "This responsibility for the Other is structured as the one-for-the-other, indeed even as the one *hostage* of the other, hostage in his very identity as irreplaceably called, before any return to self. For the other in the guise of oneself, right up to *substitution* for the Other."

32. Ibid., 21.

33. Ibid., 25–26.

34. This is the text "Knowledge of the Unknown," first published in *La nouvelle revue française*, no. 108 (1961, 1081–95,

then again in 1969 in *L'entretien infini,* translated as Maurice Blanchot, *The Infinite Conversation,* trans. Susan Hanson (Minneapolis: University of Minnesota Press, 1993), 51–52.

35. See *The Infinite Conversation,* 50–51:

— . . . I will add that if we are able to have commerce with this unknowable, it is precisely in fear or in anguish, or in one of those ecstatic movements that you just refused as being non-philosophical; it is there that we have some presentiment of the Other—it seizes us, staggers and ravishes us, carrying us away from ourselves.

—But precisely in order to change us into the Other. If in knowledge—even dialectical knowledge, and through any intermediary one might want—there is appropriation of an object by a subject and of the other by the same, and thus finally a reduction of the unknown to the already known, there is in the rapture of fright something worse; for it is the self that is lost and the same that is altered, shamefully transformed into something other than myself.

36. See *Dieu, la mort et le temps,* 134: "It is my mortality, my condemnation to death, my time on the verge of death, my death not as the possibility of impossibility but as pure rapture, that constitute the absurdity that makes possible the gratuitousness of my responsibility for the Other."

37. *The Infinite Conversation,* 51–52.

38. See *Totality and Infinity,* 86–88: "The Other measures me with a gaze incomparable to the gaze by which I discover him. The dimension of *height* in which the Other is placed is as it were the primary curvature of being from which the privilege of the Other results, the gradient of transcendence. The Other is metaphysical. . . . The relationship with the Other does not move (as does cognition) into enjoyment and possession, into freedom; the Other imposes himself as an exigency that dominates this freedom, and hence as more primordial than everything that takes place in me. . . . The presence of the Other, a privileged heteronomy, does not clash with freedom but invests it."

39. See ibid., 89: "The term welcome of the Other expresses a simultaneity of activity and passivity which places the relation with the other outside of the dichotomies valid for things: the a priori and the a posteriori, activity and passivity. But we wish to show also how, starting from knowing identified with

thematization, the truth of this knowing leads back to the relation with the Other, that is, to justice."

40. Ibid., 305: "To posit being as Desire and as goodness is not to first isolate an I which would then tend toward a beyond. It is to affirm that to apprehend oneself from within—to produce oneself as I—is to apprehend oneself with the same gesture that already turns toward the exterior to extra-vert and to manifest—to respond for what it apprehends—to express; it is to affirm that the becoming-conscious is already language, that the essence of language is goodness, or again, that the essence of language is friendship and hospitality."

41. A reference to *The Theory of Intuition in Husserl's Phenomenology*, Levinas's dissertation for the *doctorat de troisième cycle*, defended and published in 1930.

42. Emmanuel Levinas, *Théorie de l'intuition dans la phénoménologie de Husserl* (Paris: Vrin, 1970), 7; *The Theory of Intuition in Husserl's Phenomenology*, trans. André Orianne (Evanston: Northwestern University Press, 2d ed., 1995). [As the translator notes (xlix), Levinas's short preface or *avant-propos*, from which the above quote was taken, was omitted from the translation and replaced by the translator's foreword so as to provide a series of "historical remarks more specifically directed to today's English reader."—Trans.]

43. *The Theory of Intuition in Husserl's Phenomenology*, lvi.

44. Ibid., lv.

45. Ibid., lvi.

46. See, e.g., *Dieu, la mort et le temps*, 133: "Does not the traumatism of the other come from the *Other*?"

47. It is tempting to suggest that a large part of Derrida's text "At This Very Moment in This Work Here I Am" might be read as a long commentary on this expression, in relation to both Levinas's use and interpretation of it and Derrida's own critical perspective. As for Levinas, a note in *Otherwise than Being or Beyond Essence* [trans. Alphonso Lingis (The Hague: Martinus Nijhoff, 1981), n. 11 on 199] refers back explicitly to Isaiah 6: 8: Then I heard the voice of the Lord saying, 'Whom shall I send, and who will go for us?' And I said, 'Here I am; send me!'" Note that in the Septuagint the Greek equivalent of

the Hebraic *hineni* is: *idou egō* (translated literally, "here is I"), where the personal pronoun is in the nominative. The meaning of the pronoun "I" in the accusative as related to responsibility for the Other is explained by Levinas in *Otherwise than Being or Beyond Essence* (141–42):

> The subject in responsibility is alienated in the depths of its identity with an alienation that does not empty the same of its identity, but constrains it to it, with an unimpeachable assignation, constrains it to it as no one else, where no one could replace it. The psyche, a uniqueness outside of concepts, is a seed of folly, already a psychosis. It is not an ego, but me under assignation. There is an assignation to an identity for the response of responsibility, where one cannot have oneself replaced without fault. To this command continually put forth only a "here I am" (*me voici*) can answer, where the pronoun "I" is in the accusative, declined before any declension, possessed by the other, sick, identical. Here I am—is saying with inspiration, which is not a gift for fine words or songs. There is constraint to give with full hands, and thus a constraint to corporeality.

48. *Dieu, la mort et le temps*, 16.

49. See ibid., 134: "This question—the question of death—is its own response to itself: it is my responsibility for the death of the other. The passage to the ethical level constitutes the response to this question. The version of the Same toward the Infinite, which is neither aim [*visée*] nor vision, is the *question*, a question that is also a response, but in no sense a dialogue of the soul with itself. Question, prayer—does this not come before all dialogue?"

50. "Bad Conscience and the Inexorable," 39–40. "Infinity would have no meaning for a thought that goes to the limit, and the *à-Dieu* is not a finality. It is perhaps this irreducibility of the *à-Dieu* or of the fear of God to eschatology, an irreducibility that interrupts within the human the consciousness that was on its way toward being in its ontological perseverance or toward death which it takes as the ultimate thought, that is signified, beyond being, by the word 'glory.' The alternative between being and nothingness is not ultimate."

51. Ibid., 40.

A Word of Welcome

1. *Enseignement magistral* also refers to a lecture style of teaching.—Trans.

2. "Host" and "guest" are in English in the original.—Trans.

3. Emile Benveniste, *Indo-European Language and Society*, trans. Elizabeth Palmer (Coral Gables, Florida: University of Miami Press, 1973), 71ff.

4. Emmanuel Levinas, *Totality and Infinity*, trans. Alphonso Lingis (Pittsburgh: Duquesne University Press, 1969), 51. For this understanding of the Master, the "welcoming of the master," and the "welcoming of the Other," see also 100–101 and passim. The concept of *expression* is determined by the same logic of teaching and "receiving." "To receive the given is already to receive it as taught—as an expression of the Other" (92). [Throughout, we have silently altered this and other translations where necessary to better reflect what Derrida is discussing in the French original.—Trans.]

5. During the summer of 1996 some three hundred illegal immigrants of African descent (the so-called *sans-papiers*, immigrants without proper papers) took refuge in the Church of St. Bernard in Paris in order to avoid expulsion from France and to protest recently enacted immigration policies. On August 23, police stormed the church and took the protesters into custody. Some were sent back to their country of origin, while others, after a good deal of media coverage and public protest, were ultimately allowed to remain in France.—Trans.

6. *Totality and Infinity*, 299. My emphasis.

7. Ibid., 93.

8. I have tried to demonstrate this elsewhere, by means of a somewhat different path, in a discussion of decisionism in the work of Carl Schmitt. By speaking of a "passive decision," of an "unconscious decision," of a "decision of the other," and of what "to give in the name, to give to the name, of the other" might mean, I tried to argue that "a theory of the subject is incapable of accounting for the slightest decision" (*Politics of Friendship*, trans. George Collins [New York: Verso Press, 1997], 68–69). I there referred—so as to try to put it into question—

to the traditional and predominant way of determining the subject, the one that Schmitt himself, among so many others, seems to assume. It is obviously not the one that Levinas privileges when he redefines subjectivity, as we will see in a moment.

9. In the section of "No Identity" entitled "Subjectivity and Vulnerability," in *Collected Philosophical Papers*, trans. Alphonso Lingis (Dordrecht, The Netherlands: Martinus Nijhoff, 1987), 146.

10. *Totality and Infinity*, 51. "The notion of the face . . . signifies the philosophical priority of the existent over Being, an exteriority that does not call for power or possession, an exteriority that is not reducible, as with Plato, to the interiority of memory, and yet safeguards the I who welcomes it."
Such a "safeguard" of course becomes the name and the place of all the problems to follow, just as much as the welcoming, an-archy, anachrony, and infinite dissymmetry commanded by the transcendence of the Other. What about the "I," safe and sound, in the unconditional welcoming of the Other? What about its survival, its immunity, and its safety in the ethical subjection of this other subjectivity?

11. Ibid., 80.

12. Ibid., 93.

13. Ibid., 85.

14. Ibid., 82, my emphasis. "*We call justice this face to face approach, in discourse,*" says Levinas (71), who underscores this sentence and thus seems to define justice *before* the emergence of the third. But is there any place here for this "before"?

15. *Otherwise than Being or Beyond Essence*, trans. Alphonso Lingis (The Hague: Martinus Nijhoff, 1981), 150. *Totality and Infinity* already welcomes, with such words, the "ineluctable" occurrence of the third as "language" and as "justice." Cf., for example, 213, 305, etc. We will return to this below.

16. *Otherwise than Being or Beyond Essence*, 67, 191 n. 2.

17. Ibid., 157. The "contradiction in the Saying" perhaps stems from this inevitability (both fortunate and unfortunate), from this Law of substitution, from substitution as Law: the third interrupts (distances) without interrupting (distancing)

the face to face with the irreplaceable singularity of the other. That is why Levinas speaks here of distancing ("the other and the third . . . put distance between me and the other and the third")—and this is justice—though he had written in *Totality and Infinity* (71), "*We call justice this face to face approach, in discourse.*"

18. This is one of the recurring themes in the two essays I have previously devoted to Levinas's work: "Violence and Metaphysics," in *Writing and Difference*, trans. Alan Bass (Chicago: University of Chicago Press, 1978), 79–153, and "At This Very Moment in This Work Here I Am," trans. Ruben Berezdivin, in *Re-Reading Levinas*, ed. Robert Bernasconi and Simon Critchley (Bloomington: Indiana University Press, 1991), 11–48.

19. "Peace and Proximity," trans. Peter Atterton and Simon Critchley, in *Emmanuel Levinas: Basic Philosophical Writings*, ed. Adriaan T. Peperzak, Simon Critchley, and Robert Bernasconi (Bloomington: Indiana University Press, 1996), 168. Levinas underscores only the word "unique."

20. "In its ethical position, the self is distinct from the citizen born of the City, and from the individual who precedes all order in his natural egoism, from whom political philosophy, since Hobbes, tries to derive—or succeeds in deriving—the social or political order of the City" ("Useless Suffering," trans. Richard Cohen in *The Provocation of Levinas: Rethinking the Other*, ed. Robert Bernasconi and David Wood [New York: Routledge, 1988], 165).

21. French *parjure*, like English "perjury," denotes the deliberate or willful giving of false or misleading testimony before a court of law, but it is also often used outside a strictly legal context and is not so closely tied as its English counterpart to the willful intent to deceive. *Parjure* can thus be used to describe the breaking of just about any oath or obligation, whether intentionally or not, and so can be applied to acts of treason, betrayal, or infidelity, to breaches of promise, faith, or trust.—Trans.

22. *Totality and Infinity*, 201–2.

23. We are here closer than it might seem to certain state-

ments in *Totality and Infinity* that explicitly situate the will in terms of a *betrayal* that is always possible: "The will essentially violable harbors *betrayal* in its own essence" (229); "The will thus moves between its *betrayal* and its fidelity which, *simultaneous*, describe the very originality of its power" (231). My emphasis.

24. For example, *Totality and Infinity*, 51, 82, 85, 88, 89, 93, 100, 155, 300, etc.

25. Ibid., 155. My emphasis.

26. Ibid. *You* and *thou* are the only words underscored by Levinas.

27. Ibid., 155–56. My emphasis.

28. "The absoluteness of the presence of the other, which has justified our interpreting the exceptional uprightness of thou-saying as an epiphany of him, is not the simple presence in which in the last analysis things are also present" (the section of "Meaning and Sense" entitled "The Trace," in *Collected Philosophical Papers*, 106). This text situates an *illeity* beyond being, a "*third person* that is not definable by the oneself, by ipseity." The *il* of this *illeity* is marked by irreversibility and by an "unrectitude" that here seems to have no negative connotation. A certain "rectitude," on the contrary, might in fact reduce the transcendence of this *illeity*. See 103–4.

29. *Totality and Infinity*, 157.

30. Ibid., 258.

31. Ibid., 260–61.

32. *Existence and Existents*, trans. Alphonso Lingis (The Hague: Martinus Nijhoff, 1978); *Time and the Other*, trans. Richard A. Cohen (Pittsburgh: Duquesne University Press, 1987).

33. *Existence and Existents*, 84–85.

34. *Time and the Other*, 84–87.

35. *Totality and Infinity*, 254. My emphasis.

36. Franz Rosenzweig, *The Star of Redemption*, trans. William W. Hallo (Notre Dame: Notre Dame University Press, 1985), 300. Levinas also cites this verse from Leviticus (25: 23) in the section of "No Identity" entitled "Foreignness to Being," in

Collected Philosophical Papers: "No land will be alienated irrevocably, for the earth is mine, for you are but strangers, domiciled in my land" (148).

37. "At This Very Moment in This Work Here I Am." As noted above, Levinas will return to the logic of these propositions, in particular, in 1985: "At the time of my little book entitled *Time and the Other*, I thought that femininity was a modality of alterity—this 'other genre,' this 'other gender'—and that sexuality and eroticism were this non-indifference to the other, irreducible to the formal alterity of the terms taken together as a whole. I today think that it is necessary to go back even further and that the exposure, the nakedness, and the 'imperative request' of the face of the Other constitute a modality that the feminine already presupposes: the proximity of the neighbor is non-formal alterity" (remarks recorded in February 1985 in the Zurich weekly *Construire* by L. Adert and J.-Ch. Aeschlimann). But already in *Otherwise than Being or Beyond Essence* a new phenomenology of the skin, of its exposure to being wounded or caressed, situates a "responsibility before eros" (192 n. 27).

38. "The relationship established between lovers in voluptuosity . . . is the very contrary of the social relation. It excludes the third, it remains intimacy, dual solitude, closed society, the supremely non-public. The feminine is the other refractory to society, member of a dual society, an intimate society, a society without language" (*Totality and Infinity*, 264–65).

39. Ibid., 157. My emphasis.

40. Ibid., 157–58.

41. A word that Levinas once wrote with an *a*, in 1968, in the first version of "Substitution" (in the *Revue Philosophique de Louvain* 66, no. 91 [1968]: 491). The word "ess*a*nce" also appears in *De Dieu qui vient à l'idée* (Paris: Librairie Philosophique J. Vrin, 1982), 164.

42. *Totality and Infinity*, 304.

43. Here Derrida alludes to a phrase of Charles Péguy: "In the history of thought, Descartes will always be the French knight who took off at such a good pace." See "Note conjointe

sur M. Descartes et la philosophie cartésienne," in *Charles Péguy: Oeuvres en Prose* (Paris: Editions de la Pléiade, 1961), 1359.

44. *Beyond the Verse: Talmudic Readings and Lectures*, trans. Gary D. Mole (London: The Athlone Press, 1994), 195.

45. *Totality and Infinity*, 24.

46. Ibid., 305.

47. *Archives de philosophie*, vol. 34, no. 3 (July-September 1971): 388, reprinted in *Otherwise than Being or Beyond Essence*, 193 n. 35.

48. See, for example, *Otherwise than Being or Beyond Essence*, 183. [In the following paragraph Derrida cites 193 and 94.—Trans.]

49. *Totality and Infinity*, 298: "We have thus the conviction of having broken with the philosophy of the Neuter: with the Heideggerian Being of the existent whose impersonal neutrality the critical work of Blanchot has so much contributed to bring out."

Since the thought of the Neuter, as it continues to be elaborated in the work of Blanchot, can in no way be reduced to what Levinas understands here by the Neuter, an enormous and abyssal task remains open. Levinas himself suggests this, much later, precisely on the subject of the Neuter and the *there is* [il y a]: "I think Maurice Blanchot's work and thought can be interpreted in two directions at the same time" ("On Maurice Blanchot," in *Proper Names*, trans. Michael B. Smith [Stanford: Stanford University Press, 1996], 154). Yes, in at least two directions.

50. *Totality and Infinity*, 154–56. These analyses are developed in an at once fascinating and problematic way in the chapter "Phenomenology of Eros." They were already announced in the lectures of 1946–47 gathered together under the title *Time and the Other*. As we have already emphasized, the difference between the sexes is analyzed there beyond "some specific difference," as a "formal structure." Beyond "contradiction" or "the duality of two complementary terms," it "carves up reality in another sense and conditions the very possibility of reality as

multiple, against the unity of being proclaimed by Parmenides" (85–86). Destined to hide, to "a flight before the light" and to "modesty," femininity represents everything in alterity that resists concealment/unconcealment, or veiling/unveiling, that is, a certain determination of truth. It is, in truth, alterity itself: "alterity is accomplished in the feminine" (87–88).

51. "Openness can be understood in several senses," we read in the section of "No Identity" entitled "Subjectivity and Vulnerability," in *Collected Philosophical Papers*, 145. The first has to do with the openness of an object to every other object (a reference to Kant's third analogy of experience in *The Critique of Pure Reason*); the second concerns intentionality or the ecstasy of ek-sistence (Husserl and Heidegger). The "third meaning" is more important for Levinas; it concerns the "denuding of the skin exposed," the "vulnerability of a skin exposed, in wounds and outrage, beyond all that can show itself," "sensibility" "offered to the caress," but also "open like a city declared open upon the approach of the enemy." Unconditional hospitality would be this vulnerability—at once passive, exposed, *and* assumed.

52. *Totality and Infinity*, 300.

53. Ibid., 299.

54. *Otherwise than Being or Beyond Essence*, 112.

55. Ibid., 114. See also 117, 128, 141, 158, 167.

56. This allusion to a passage from Lamentations (3: 30) is found elsewhere in a very discreet contestation of its Christian reinscription, a pathetic, mortified, indeed masochistic reinscription: "Vulnerability is more (or less) than passivity receiving a form or a shock. . . . 'He offered his cheek to the smiters and was filled with shame,' says, admirably, a prophetic text. Without introducing a deliberate searching for suffering or humiliation (turning the other cheek), it suggests, in the primary suffering, in suffering as such, an unendurable and harsh consent that animates the passivity and does so strangely despite itself, although passivity as such has neither force nor intention, and no likes or dislikes" (the section of "No Identity" entitled "Subjectivity and Vulnerability," in *Collected Philosophical Papers*, 146).

57. *Otherwise than Being or Beyond Essence*, 111–12.

58. Permit me to refer once again to Benveniste's analyses in the chapter of *Indo-European Language and Society* devoted to hospitality. They would also call for a reading and for numerous questions that must for the moment be left in suspense.

59. *Otherwise than Being or Beyond Essence*, 118.

60. Ibid., 112.

61. Ibid., 123. The preceding page gave an affirmative answer to this question of the link between the election and the responsibility of the unique subject, unique and irreplaceable, paradoxically, insofar as it is subject to substitution. "Has not the Good chosen the subject with an election recognizable in the responsibility of being hostage, to which the subject is destined, which he cannot evade without denying himself, and by virtue of which he is unique?" The analysis of this situation takes into account an absolute "lateness" that dethrones the authority of the present or of anamnesic presentation, that limits the freedom but not the responsibility of the moral subject (of Job, for example, who can be responsible for an evil he "never wished"), and that makes this entire logic of the hostage depend on the unconditionality of a *yes* that is older than infantile or pre-critical spontaneity, a *yes* as "the very exposure to critique."

Descartes had already been called to appear, called to *bear witness* ("the unimpeachable witness of Descartes's Third Meditation") in *Totality and Infinity*, precisely at the moment of the reinscription of the *ego cogito*: a subject subjected to its election, responsible for having to respond, secondarily, *yes* to a first *yes*, to this first call that, as we said above, like every *yes*, even if it is the first, already *responds*: "The I in the negativity manifested by doubt breaks with participation but does not find in the *cogito* itself a stopping place. It is not I, it is the other that can say *yes*. From him comes affirmation; he is at the commencement of experience. Descartes seeks a certitude, and stops at the first change of level in this vertiginous descent. . . . to possess the idea of infinity is to have already welcomed the Other" (*Totality and Infinity*, 93). To have welcomed this *yes* of the other, to greet this infinity in separation, or to say it otherwise, in its ho-liness, is the experience of the *à-Dieu*. The *Adieu* does not wait for death but calls, responds and greets in the relation with the other insofar as it *is* not, insofar as it calls from beyond being. To God [*A Dieu*] beyond being, where the *yes* of faith is not in-compatible with a certain atheism or at least with a *certain* thought of the *inexistence* of God (beyond being). We will look more closely later at the use Levinas was able to make of this word *à-Dieu*. Though the experience of the *à-Dieu* can remain silent, it is no less irrecusable. It is from within this experience that we speak here, even when we speak in a whisper, and it is toward it that we will return, toward this infinitely difficult thought to which Levinas gave, in the French language and by means of its idiom, with its idiom as destination, an excep-tional chance, a rare economy, one that is, in a word, at once unique, more than old, inaugural, and yet also replaceable: al-ways translatable by paraphrases, of course, and as such always exposed to inanities.

62. *Totality and Infinity*, 213. The question of the third was not only present, as we see, but developed in *Totality and In-finity*. One is thus a bit surprised by the concession Levinas seems to make to one of his interlocutors during an interview. On the question of the third and justice, he seems to admit that *Totality and Infinity* did not adequately treat these themes: "the word 'justice' applies much more to the relation with the third than to the relation with the Other. But in reality the relation with the Other is never uniquely the relation with the Other: the third is represented in the Other from the very beginning; in the very apparition of the Other the third already looks at me, already concerns me. . . . You are right, in any case, to make this distinction. The ontological language used in *Total-ity and Infinity* is not at all definitive. In *Totality and Infinity* language is ontological because it wants above all to avoid be-ing psychological" (*De Dieu qui vient à l'idée*, 132–33).

63. "God and Philosophy," in *Collected Philosophical Papers*, 165.

64. *Otherwise than Being or Beyond Essence*, 121. My emphasis.

65. In the section of "Meaning and Sense" entitled "The Trace," in *Collected Philosophical Papers*, 106.

66. Ibid., 106–7.

67. *In the Time of the Nations*, trans. Michael B. Smith (London: The Athlone Press, 1994), 97.

68. *Beyond the Verse*, 193.

69. I have tried to express this in a general fashion but with particular emphasis on Levinas's thought on fraternity (cf. *Politics of Friendship*, 304–5). Levinas here comes close to, among many others, the Kant of the *The Doctrine of Virtue* [see "The Ethical Doctrine of Elements" in the "The Doctrine of Virtue," *The Metaphysics of Morals*, second part, sections 46–47, trans. Mary J. Gregor (Cambridge: Cambridge University Press, 1991)]. I analyze this relation at some length (*Politics of Friendship*, 252–63), and suggest that "the determination of friendship *qua fraternity*. . . tells us something essential about ethics."

Kant: "All men are as brothers under one universal father who wills the happiness of all."

Levinas: "The very status of the human implies fraternity and the idea of the human race. . . . it involves the commonness of a father, as though the commonness of race would not bring together enough" (*Totality and Infinity*, 214).

To trace the destiny of this fraternity beyond the family, all the way to the order of justice and the political, one must take into account what Levinas says, as if in passing, about the non-coincidence with unicity and thus with the self. This is the irruption of equality, and thus already of the third: "It is my responsibility before a face looking at me as absolutely foreign (and the epiphany of the face coincides with these two moments) that constitutes the original fact of fraternity. Paternity is not a causality, but the establishment of a unicity with which the unicity of the father does and does not coincide. The non-coincidence consists, concretely, in my position as brother; it implies other unicities at my side. Thus my unicity *qua* I contains both self-sufficiency of being and my partialness, my position before the other as a face. In this welcoming of the face . . . equality is founded. It cannot be detached from the welcoming of the face, of which it is a moment" (*Totality and Infinity*, 214).

It would also be necessary to follow the later development of this analysis in "Transcendence and Fecundity" and, especially, in "Filiality and Fraternity." Filiality is there determined before all else as—or indeed only as—the "father-son relationship." It again inscribes equality within election: "each son of the father is the unique son, the chosen son. . . . a *unique* child, an only child." It is by virtue of this "strange conjuncture of the family" that "fraternity is the very relation with the face in which at the same time my election and equality . . . are accomplished." Next comes the deduction of the "third" and of the socio-political "We" that "encompasses the structure of the family itself" (*Totality and Infinity*, 278–80). See also *Otherwise than Being or Beyond Essence*, 140, 152, and *passim*: "the structure of the-one-for-the-other inscribed in human fraternity, in the one keeper of his brother, the one responsible for the other"—this is what would have remained "unintelligible for Plato, and had to lead him to commit a parricide on his father Parmenides"; "The unity of the human race is in fact posterior to fraternity" (166).

70. *In the Time of the Nations*, 97.

71. This discourse of substitution is to be read from out of the depths of an abyssal history. We spoke just a moment ago, citing Levinas, of a "Judeo-Christian spirituality." It will one day be necessary, so as to recall and understand Islam, to question patiently many of the affinities, analogies, synonymies and homonymies, be they the result of a crossing of paths, sometimes unbeknownst to the authors, or of necessities that are more profound, though often perplexing and oblique. The most pressing (and no doubt least noticed) example in France is to be found in another thought of substitution, one that, under this very name, traverses the entire oeuvre and adventure of Louis Massignon. Inherited from Huysmans—whom Levinas in fact evokes early on in *From Existence to Existents*, "between 1940 and 1945"—and at work throughout the tradition of a certain Christian mysticism (Bloy, Foucauld, Claudel, the author

of *The Hostage*, etc.) to which Massignon remains faithful, the word-concept "substitution" inspires in Massignon a whole thought of "sacred hospitality," a foundational reference to the hospitality of Abraham, or Ibrahim, and the institution, in 1934, of *Badaliya*—a word that belongs to the Arab vocabulary of "substitution": "these souls for which we wish to substitute ourselves '*fil badaliya*,' by paying a ransom for them at our expense, is a replacement," say the Statues of the *Badaliya*, where the word "hostages" is written in bold letters: "we offer and we commit our lives, beginning now, *as hostages*" (Louis Massignon, *L'hospitalité sacrée* [Paris: Nouvelle Cité, 1987], 373–74). *Hostage* is again written in bold letters when used in relation to the first person ("I had been made into a *hostage*"), as a letter of 1947 reveals (241). See also 171–73, 262–63, 281 ("fraternal substitution"), 300–1 and passim. Massignon's use of the word "persecution" also resonates, up to a certain point (but which one?), with Levinas's (cf., for example, 305), but on a "front of Islamo-Christian prayer." Cf. also Massignon's "Le linceul de feu d'Abraham," in *Parole donnée* (Paris: Editions du Seuil, 1983).

72. *In the Time of the Nations*, 98.

73. Ibid.   74. Ibid.

75. *Beyond the Verse*, 183.   76. Ibid., 186.

77. Ibid., 183.   78. Ibid., 177.

79. For example, in "Séparation des biens" (*Cahiers de l'Herne*, 1991, 465). There Levinas puts forward a legitimate, legal argument, no doubt (the State of Israel "includes citizens of every denomination. Its religious party is neither the only party nor the most influential one"), but those who doubt the "laicity" of this State will not be easily satisfied by this argument.

80. "Au-delà de l'Etat dans l'Etat," in *Nouvelles lectures talmudiques* (Paris: Editions de Minuit, 1996), 63.

81. Ibid., 62.

82. Ibid., 64.

83. Ibid., 48.

84. *Beyond the Verse*, 187. My emphasis.

85. Ibid., 192.   86. Ibid., 194.

87. Ibid., 195.   88. Ibid., 194.

89. Ibid., 191. My emphasis.

90. Ibid., 193–94. [In the following paragraph, Derrida relates these lines to a passage from the final section of the chapter "Substitution" in *Otherwise than Being or Beyond Essence*, 128.—Trans.]

91. *Beyond the Verse*, 150–52.

92. Immanuel Kant, *Perpetual Peace*, trans. Lewis White Beck (Indianapolis: The Bobbs-Merrill Company, Inc., 1957), 10.

93. In "Avances," preface to Serge Margel's *Le tombeau du Dieu artisan* (Paris: Editions de Minuit, 1995).

94. Among many other possible examples, see *In the Time of the Nations*, III: "The entire Torah, in its minute descriptions, is concentrated in the 'Thou shalt not kill' that the face of the other signifies, and awaits its proclamation therein."

95. To my knowledge, Levinas never speaks of Schmitt. This theoretician of the political is situated at the opposite extreme from Levinas, with all the paradoxes and reversals that such an absolute opposition might harbor. Schmitt is not only a thinker of hostility (and not of hospitality); he not only situates the enemy at the center of a "politics" that is irreducible to the ethical, if not to the juridical. He is also, by his own admission, a sort of Catholic neo-Hegelian who has an essential need to adhere to a thought of totality. This discourse of the enemy as the discourse of totality, so to speak, would thus embody for Levinas the absolute adversary. More so than Heidegger, it seems. For Heidegger does not give in either to "politism" or to the fascination of a (supposedly Hegelian) totality. The question of being, in its transcendence (*epekeina tes ousias*, a phrase that Heidegger also often cites), goes beyond the totality of beings. The passage beyond totality was thus, at least in its formality, a movement whose necessity Heidegger, no less than Rosenzweig, recognized. Whence the strained and precarious filiations of a heritage.

96. In English in the original.—Trans.

97. *Totality and Infinity*, 172.

98. Ibid.

99. Ibid., 306.

100. *Totality and Infinity*, 300, cf. also 305 and passim.

101. Ibid., 301 and passim.

102. Ibid., 300, 305.

103. Ibid., 172–73. My emphasis.

104. Ibid., 306.

105. Ibid.

106. Ibid., 300. My emphasis.

107. Ibid.

108. *Otherwise than Being or Beyond Essence*, 112.

109. *De Dieu qui vient à l'idée*, 250. [Page 11 of this text is cited in the passage just above.—Trans.]

110. Ibid., 12. My emphasis.

111. For example, after having named the devotion of the *à-Dieu* (see above: "A way of being destined or devoted that is devotion itself"), Levinas continues: "A devotion that, in its dis-inter-estedness, does not fail to reach a goal, but is diverted—by a God 'who loves the stranger' rather than shows himself—toward the other man for whom I am responsible. Responsibility without concern for reciprocity: I have to be responsible for the Other without concerning myself about the Other's responsibility toward me. Relation without correlation or love of the neighbor, a love without eros. For-the-other man and, through this, *à-Dieu*!" (*De Dieu qui vient à l'idée*, 12–13). Or again: "But the commitment from this 'profound past' of the immemorial comes back to me as order and demand, as commandment, in the face of the other man, of a God 'who loves the stranger,' of an invisible, non-thematizable God. . . . Infinity to which I am destined or devoted by a non-intentional thought for which no preposition in our language—not even the *à* [to] to which we resort—would be able to translate the devotion. *A-Dieu* whose diachronic time is the only measure, the unique number [*chiffre unique*], at once devotion and transcendence" (ibid., 250).

112. *Beyond the Verse*, 52.

113. Regarding this chapter, see Daniel Payot's *Des villes-refuges: Témoignage et espacement* (La Tour d'Aigues: Editions l'Aube, 1992). I treat this from another angle in *Cosmopolites de tous les pays, encore un effort!* (Paris: Editions Galilée, 1997).

114. Psalms 132: 13. *New Revised Standard Version: The New Oxford Annotated Bible* (New York: Oxford University Press, 1991).

This verse is re-translated, interpreted, reinscribed, and meditated upon in *Chant d'Outre Tombe*, by Michal Govrin, in order to introduce a reading of Celan's Jerusalem ("*Sag, dass Jerusalem ist*"), in *Le passage des frontières* (Paris: Editions Galilée, 1994), 228: "A passion that has not let go of the West for some twenty-five centuries. The passion to conquer this city-woman-wound. A passionate madness . . . The desire to be in Jerusalem, to possess her . . . The desire to be the conqueror of Jerusalem, her sole possessor and lover, this exclusive passion might have as its origin and model the God of the Bible: 'Get up, Lord, so as to go into your *place of repose*. . . . For the Eternal has *made his choice* in Zion. He *desired* it as his dwelling. This will be my *place of repose for ever*. There I will dwell for I *lusted* (*ivitiha*) after her.'"

115. *Beyond the Verse*, 38.   116. Ibid., 42.
117. Ibid., 40.   118. Ibid.
119. Ibid., 43.   120. Ibid., 44.
121. Ibid., 46.   122. *Totality and Infinity*, 305.

123. For example: "The third looks at me in the eyes of the Other—language is justice. . . . The poor one, the stranger, presents himself as an equal. His equality within this essential poverty consists in referring to the *third*, thus present at the encounter, whom in the midst of his destitution the Other already serves. He comes to *join* me. But he joins me to himself for service; he commands me as a Master. . . . By essence the prophetic word responds to the epiphany of the face. . . . an irreducible moment of a discourse which by essence is aroused by the epiphany of the face inasmuch as it attests the presence of the third, the whole of humanity, in the eyes that look at me" (*Totality and Infinity*, 213).

124. See, for example, *Totality and Infinity*, 298.

125. *Beyond the Verse*, 51–52. I emphasize the words "longing" and "hope." We must be attentive here to the fact that when Levinas tries to distinguish the Jewish State from some particu-

larism or nationalism, he always speaks not of some present fact, but of a possibility, of a promise for the future, of an "aspiration," a "commitment," a "hope," or a "project." For example: "Does not the fact that the history of the Jewish people, wherein the *hope* for a Jewish State on earth was always essential, could have caused Sartre to have doubts about the sovereign and majestic architecture of Hegelian logic, also suggest that the State in question does not *open* onto a *purely political* history, the one written by the victorious and triumphant? And that such a *project*, far from suggesting a *nationalist particularism*, is one of the *possibilities* of the difficult humanity of the human?" These lines conclude a couple of pages devoted to Sartre at the time of his death ("Un langage qui nous est familier," in *Emmanuel Levinas*, Les Cahiers de la nuit surveillée [Lagrasse: Editions Verdier, 1984], 328). Levinas insists that throughout the evolution of his thought, beginning with *Réflexions sur la question juive* [trans. George J. Becker as *Anti-Semite and Jew* (New York: Schocken Books, 1948)], Sartre remained faithful to the State of Israel, "in spite of all the comprehension shown for Palestinian nationalism and its genuine sorrows" (327). To the expression "Palestinian nationalism" there will never correspond the expression "Israeli nationalism." When Levinas writes, "What Israel is inaugurating in the Holy Land is not just one more nationalism or sect" ("Séparation des biens," *Cahiers de l'Herne* [1991], 465), he nonetheless speaks of the "religious grandeur" of the Zionist project. "These days, one does not carry the Bible in one's luggage with impunity" (ibid.). But let us not forget, let us never forget, that the same Bible also travels in the luggage of Palestinians, be they Muslim or Christian. Justice and thirdness.

126. 1 Kings 19: 12–15.

127. "A priori exposed to substitution"—which is to say, perhaps, "before" all sacrifice, independently of any sacrificial experience, even if the possibility of such experience might be located here. As a word and as a concept, does this a priori (at once formal and concrete) have a place in Levinas's discourse? It is not certain. This raises the enormous question of the rela-

tionship between substitution and sacrifice, between the being-hostage, the being-host, and the sacrificial experience. Levinas often uses the word "sacrifice" to designate the "substitution which precedes the will" (*Otherwise than Being or Beyond Essence*, 127), though he relates it to its Judaic signification, that is, to the notion of an approach—"the approach, inasmuch as it is a sacrifice" (ibid., 129).

128. See the articles collected and presented by Catherine Chalier under the titles "Epreuves d'une pensée" and "Quelques réflexions sur la philosophie de l'hitlérisme," in the *Cahier de l'Herne* devoted to Levinas (ed. Catherine Chalier and Miguel Abensour [Paris: Editions de l'Herne, 1991]). [See "Reflections on the Philosophy of Hitlerism," trans. Seán Hand, *Critical Inquiry* 17 (Autumn 1990): 63–71.—Trans.]

129. "The secularization of all spiritual values during the nineteenth century gave rise both to Jewish nationalist doctrines and the easy assimilation that made possible the pure and simple disappearance of the Jew. Two ways of escaping or renouncing the fact of the diaspora; two paths that the Covenant has always refused to follow. For it remained faithful to an older vocation. By proclaiming that Judaism was only a religion, it asked of Jews more, and not less, than Jewish nationalism, and offered them a task more worthy than Judaization" ("L'inspiration religieuse de l'alliance" ["The religious Inspiration of the Covenant"], 1935, in ibid., 146).

130. Or a parable? "According to a Talmudic parable, all Jews, past, present, and future, were there at the foot of Sinai; in a certain sense, all were present at Auschwitz" ("Séparation des biens," ibid., 465).

131. From the lecture course *Sur la mort et le temps*, in ibid., 68; reprinted in *Dieu, la mort et le temps*, ed. Jacques Rolland (Paris: Grasset, 1993), 122.

132. Emmanuel Levinas, "La conscience non-intentionnelle," in *Cahiers de l'Herne*, 118–19, and in *Entre nous: Essais sur le penser-à-l'autre* (Paris: Grasset, 1991), 150. [See "Bad Conscience and the Inexorable," in *Face to Face with Levinas*, ed. Richard A. Cohen (Albany: SUNY Press, 1986), 40.—Trans.]

133. *De Dieu qui vient à l'idée*, 134.

134. Ibid., 151.

135. Once again the "marvel of the family" between—or beyond—Hegel, Kierkegaard, and Rosenzweig: "The situation in which the I thus posits itself before truth in placing its subjective morality in the infinite time of its fecundity—a situation in which the instant of eroticism and the infinity of paternity are conjoined—is concretized in the marvel of the family. The family does not only result from a rational arrangement of animality; it does not simply mark a step toward the anonymous universality of the State. It identifies itself outside of the State, even if the State reserves a framework for it" (*Totality and Infinity*, 306).

None of the questions that might be raised by these interpretations of the family and paternity should blind us to certain irreducible complications: not only, as we have noted, does the feminine-being signify, as "welcoming par excellence," the origin of ethics, but *paternity* can never be reduced to *virility*, for it is almost as if paternity disturbed the order of sexual difference within the family. We spoke earlier of this paradox: paternity is, with regard to the State, anarchy itself. The virility of heroic virtue, on the other hand, often takes on a negative connotation in its association with war and the State. Near the very end of *Totality and Infinity*, the word *virile* is used in a way that conforms to its use throughout. It is a question each time of a political and warlike courage that risks death in the *finite* time of the State, as opposed to the infinite fecundity of the father/son relation. "Situated at the antipodes of the subject living in the infinite time of fecundity is the isolated and heroic being that the State produces by its virile virtues."

136. *In the Time of the Nations*, 61. My emphasis.

MERIDIAN

Crossing Aesthetics

Hans-Jost Frey, *Studies in Poetic Discourse: Mallarmé, Baudelaire, Rimbaud, Hölderlin*

Pierre Bourdieu, *The Rules of Art: Genesis and Structure of the Literary Field*

Nicolas Abraham, *Rhythms: On the Work, Translation, and Psychoanalysis*

Jacques Derrida, *On the Name*

David Wills, *Prosthesis*

Maurice Blanchot, *The Work of Fire*

Jacques Derrida, *Points . . . : Interviews, 1974–1994*

J. Hillis Miller, *Topographies*

Philippe Lacoue-Labarthe, *Musica Ficta (Figures of Wagner)*

Jacques Derrida, *Aporias*

Emmanuel Levinas, *Outside the Subject*

Jean-François Lyotard, *Lessons on the Analytic of the Sublime*

Peter Fenves, *"Chatter": Language and History in Kierkegaard*

Jean-Luc Nancy, *The Experience of Freedom*

Jean-Joseph Goux, *Oedipus, Philosopher*

Haun Saussy, *The Problem of a Chinese Aesthetic*

Jean-Luc Nancy, *The Birth to Presence*

Library of Congress Cataloging-in-Publication Data

Derrida, Jacques
  [Adieu à Emmanuel Lévinas.   English]
  Adieu to Emmanuel Levinas / Jacques Derrida ; translated by
Pascale-Anne Brault and Michael Naas.
     p.   cm. — (Meridian, crossing aesthetics)
  Includes bibliographical references.
  ISBN 0-8047-3267-1 (hardcover : alk. paper). — ISBN 0-8047-3275-2
(pbk. : alk. paper)
    I. Lévinas, Emmanuel. I. Title. II. Series: Meridian
(Stanford, Calif.)
B2430.L484D4513   1999
194—dc21   99-21519

This book is printed on acid-free paper

Original printing 1999

Typeset by James P. Brommer
in 10.9/13 Garamond and Lithos display